JOHN PAUL JONES

America's Sailor

JOHN PAUL JONES

America's Sailor

Bruce L. Brager

MORGAN
REYNOLDS
PUBLISHING
Greensboro, North Carolina

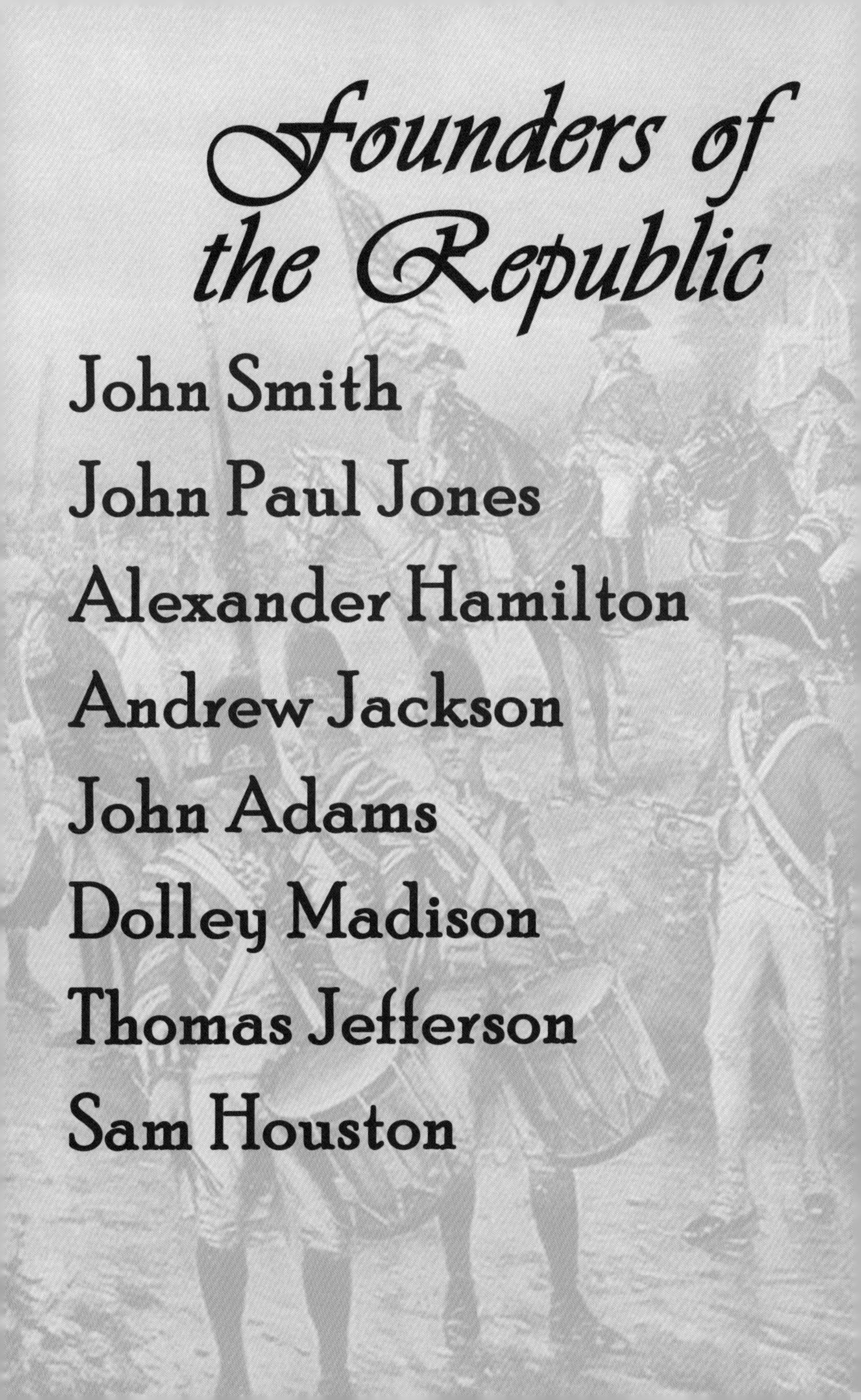

Founders of the Republic

John Smith

John Paul Jones

Alexander Hamilton

Andrew Jackson

John Adams

Dolley Madison

Thomas Jefferson

Sam Houston

JOHN PAUL JONES: AMERICA'S SAILOR

Morgan Reynolds Publishing, Inc., 620 South Elm Street, Suite 223
Greensboro, North Carolina 27406 USA

Library of Congress Cataloging-in-Publication Data

Brager, Bruce L., 1949-
John Paul Jones : America's sailor / Bruce L. Brager.— 1st ed.
p. cm.
Includes bibliographical references and index.
ISBN-13: 978-1-931798-84-6 (library binding)
ISBN-10: 1-931798-84-2 (library binding)
1. Jones, John Paul, 1747-1792—Juvenile literature. 2. Admirals—United States—Biography—Juvenile literature. 3. United States. Navy—Biography—Juvenile literature. 4. United States—History—Revolution, 1775-1783—Naval operations—Juvenile literature. I. Title.
E207.J7B82 2006
973.3'5092—dc22

2005030443

Printed in the United States of America
First Edition

Contents

One

Beginnings and Implications

John Paul Jones, the classic example of the self-made man, even chose his name. He was born John Paul, on July 6, 1747, at Kirkbean, a seacoast town in western Scotland, the youngest of five children, with an older brother and three older sisters. His father, John Paul Sr., was what today would be called a landscape architect, a trained professional, but then was known as a gardener. John Sr. had been recruited all the way from Scotland's east coast to design and construct the formal gardens at the estate of Arbigland. This was a good time for landscape gardening in Great Britain, with plenty of large landowners wanting planned gardens on their estates. John Sr. designed the gardens and provided maintenance for them as well as the house,

Opposite: *John Paul Jones.* (U.S. Senate)

while supervising a staff of one hundred workers.

Despite his experience and skill, John Sr. was a member of the serving class and would always remain one. In the stratified society of the time, he always had to defer to the lord of the estate, William Craik, who made certain he was treated as a lord should be treated by his help. Craik's daughter described her father as "ardent to make himself completely master of whatever he took in hand."

The people of Scotland had lived with a hefty burden for generations: the sometimes oppressive arm of the British government to the south. Occasionally, the Scots would rise in rebellion, only to be thwarted by the superior English army. The year before John Paul Jr. was born, the English had brutally crushed the last and most famous rebellion, led by Charles Edward Stuart, "Bonnie Prince Charlie." While Craik had supported the English, Paul's mother, Jean McDuff, a highland Scot from an area most supportive of the prince, quietly hoped Prince Charles would succeed.

John Jr. might have inherited his lifelong resentment of the English from his mother, though it is not known whether her family had any direct involvement in the rebellion. His psychological inheritance from his father came from having to watch a talented, gifted man be visibly subservient to Craik, who had gained his position by birth, not talent. John Sr. never openly defied Craik, but it would not be surprising if his resentment was shared with his son. John Paul Jr. might also have wondered whether his father had another reason to resent Craik. Some historians have speculated that Paul might have been Craik's illegitimate son. No real evidence exists, but Craik had a reputation as a womanizer and had produced at least one illegitimate son—who later in life became George Washington's personal physician.

John Jr. and his family lived in a small cottage overlooking the Firth of Solway. This inlet, part of the Irish Sea, divides England and Scotland. When the weather was clear, John Jr. could see England across the water; ships sailed in and out of the firth. He liked to play admiral, standing on a rock on the shore yelling orders to playmates in rowboats. His love of the sea was part of him from birth.

John Paul Jr. wanted more than just to go to sea. He wanted to join the British Royal Navy, the most powerful navy in the world. The Royal Navy was one of the few paths for advancement available to boys of John Paul's class. But it was difficult to get a foot on even this low-level step. Most of those who entered as "midshipmen," essentially officer-trainees aboard naval vessels, had good social connections, even if they did not have the social standing themselves. Many midshipmen were sons of aristocracy who would not inherit the family title or money.

John Paul Jr.'s family did not have these connections, but he did the best he could. At age thirteen, a common age for entering a career at sea at the time, he signed on as an apprentice on a merchant ship. Apprenticeship was a system of on-the-job training common at the time. Spe-

This eighteenth-century map of the British Isles shows the western coast of Scotland. John Paul Jones's hometown was near the Firth of Solway. (Library of Congress)

cific conditions would vary by profession and by case—ranging from virtual servitude to being nearly a member of the family—but generally a boy would agree to work for a master for seven years with little or no pay. In return, the apprentice would learn the master's trade or profession.

Paul agreed to spend seven years at a low-level job on a ship while learning the arts of the seaman, including the critical skill of navigation. If he had the ability and drive, he might eventually become the captain of a merchant vessel. But this was still not the same as being a naval officer.

John's first ship, the *Friendship,* was a two-masted brig, a small vessel. All vessels at the time were powered by sail or by oars. (John Fitch made the first successful voyage on a steamboat in 1787, on the Delaware River.) The *Friendship* stretched about eighty feet long, with a total cargo capacity of less than two hundred tons.

The *Friendship* would give someone new a quick and drastic introduction to the sea. While there is little documentation available about life on the *Friendship,* we can assume that John's ship would roll and bounce constantly, particularly in its home waters of the wintry Irish Sea. Seasickness affected all but the most experienced seamen. Abigail Adams, whose husband John Paul would come to know, described seasickness as "that most disheartening, dispiriting malady. . . . No person, who is a stranger to the sea, can form an adequate idea of the debility occasioned by sea-sickness."

Seasickness was probably a minor concern compared

Two-masted brigs such as the Friendship *were commonly used in the eighteenth century to carry cargo.* (Courtesy of Art Resource.)

to other things young John Paul had to adjust to. In the age of sailing—roughly the mid-sixteenth century to the mid-nineteenth century—relatively small vessels were at the mercy of the weather. Even under good weather with a fair wind, the crew of the *Friendship* would have to work hard to keep the canvas sails in good condition, unfurled on wooden masts, and properly positioned to take advantage of the wind. Sailors had to climb onto the mast, and along the cross beams, known as spars, to adjust the sails. This delicate work was performed at heights up to one hundred feet above the deck. In any sort of bad weather, which was particularly common in the North Atlantic, the ship could be rolling from side to side and bouncing as sailors slipped up and along the ship's mast and spars. The ship's movement would be magnified at the top of the swaying mast. A sailor at the top of the mast in a storm could find himself whipped dizzyingly back and forth and from side to side, as if he were on a berserk amusement park ride.

A sailor who fell off a mast would hit a wooden deck and likely be killed from the force of the landing. If he fell into the water, he would probably drown. It was hard to turn around a sailing vessel, and the water of the North Atlantic was cold enough to kill a man in a just a few minutes. Surprisingly, most sailors of the day did not know how to swim.

Those who survived smashing into the deck would be at the mercy of doctors. Though a vaccine for smallpox had recently been developed, the medicine of the time was otherwise rudimentary. Doctors knew little about sanitation and would often amputate a broken limb to prevent death by gangrene. The injured could only pray that if maggots appeared on the wound, it would occur to the ship's doctor (if there was one) to leave them there to eat away the rotting flesh and infection.

Though the food was likely to provide sufficient calories for the rigorous life at sea, the menu started out poor and, as fresh food was used up while the ship was at sea, got worse during the voyage. Meat was preserved in brine (salt water). Fresh vegetables or fruit were impossible to keep. Dried peas were rock hard and biscuits were usually full of insects called weevils. Sailors would save the bread for later and then try to eat in the dark to avoid watching it move as they ate it. Butter turned rancid and tasted like grease. The British Royal Navy packed limes on its ships for the sailors to suck to avoid scurvy (a disease caused by a lack of vitamin C, which is most often found in citrus fruit), giving the nickname "Limey" to the British ever since. But many merchant captains did not make the investment. Many captains would try to catch fish, if circumstances permitted, adding some variety to the dismal food.

Officers ate better than the men, sometimes getting fresh meat, primarily pork and chicken, from animals kept on board. Some sailors disliked attending to animals meant for others to eat. Protests, or refusal to carry out orders, could result in a sailor receiving tough discipline. This could include flogging—being whipped on the bare back with a "cat o' nine tails," which is a multi-corded whip with each "tail" tied into a knot.

Drinking water developed a layer of slime after some weeks at sea. Sailors compensated for this with a daily allowance of alcohol, even for teenage apprentices. A famous beverage was "grog," made from four ounces of rum and four ounces of water. A man with a headache from grog would be called "groggy." If the groggy headache, or general seasickness, caused a man to throw up, he might use either the side of the ship or the "head." The head was a bathroom-like facility, really just a board with holes which emptied into the ocean below. Often, particularly in bad weather when most of the crew were below decks, the men would relieve themselves where they stood. The bilge water, collecting at the bottom of the vessel, would be an indescribably horrible mess. The smell below decks, taking into account that there was insufficient fresh water to bathe, was equally bad.

Because of the difficult conditions, desertion was a constant problem. In order to have enough men, captains would sometimes be reduced to "impressment," dragging men off the streets and forcing them to serve. But the sea also had a romantic appeal to many, and life on land could be even tougher for thc lower classes.

John Paul moved up in rank when he learned navigation. He was given a brass navigator's tool called an octant (a pie-shaped instrument with a lever for measuring angles), shown how to use it, and told to plot the position of the ship. Determining the north/south position of the ship was not that difficult, as long as the sun was out. Officers would use the octant to determine the angle of the sun, check special tables, and know roughly the north/south position of the ship. At night, navigators could check the stars to determine north/south position.

East/west position was much harder find. A system that used a clock and indicators of speed enabled sailors to plot east/west position. Mariners developed a system of "knots," in which a rope with knots tied at specific

An eighteenth-century sailor holds an octant, a navigational instrument with an artificial horizon in the form of a pendulum. (Historic Coast & Geodetic Survey Collection, NOAA)

intervals was fed overboard. Someone at the back of the ship counted the number of knots that passed over in a certain amount of time. For example, five knots in thirty seconds meant the ship was traveling at five knots per hour. A knot works out to a little over one mile per hour.

Because navigation was difficult and because maps were often incomplete or unreliable, officers had to use a combination of skill and intuition to guide their ships. Bad weather, especially when ships were near land, increased the chances that a boat and its crew could be lost or wrecked.

Despite these hardships, John Paul knew he had picked the right career. The sea was his element. But there would be obstacles, some self-imposed, on his career that had to be overcome before he began his rise to fame.

Two

Early Maritime Career

Young John Paul went to sea because it offered him the best chance to improve his station in life. It might even bring him wealth and fame. He and the sea were a good match. It was a place that revealed character, particularly the ability to pay attention to details. Ships depended for their very survival on accuracy. If the man standing watch failed to notice the first faint signs of a reef, for example, he might be responsible for the destruction of his vessel and the deaths of all on board. The officers had to be sure their men understood the importance of each job.

John Paul loved the sea because it tested him and allowed him to prove his abilities, regardless of the station of his birth. He worked on improving his image and his social skills. He tried to rid himself of his

Fredericksburg, Virginia, where Jones stayed during his first years in America. Due to its convenient position along the Rappahannock River, the town, established in 1728, served as an inland port for the colonial frontier as it moved west of the coastal plain. (Library of Congress)

Scottish brogue, which branded him as not being from the aristocratic class, and to improve his written and spoken English. He associated as much as possible with the upper classes. Most significantly for his future, he visited the British colonies in America. Records show that John spent almost the entire summer of 1762 in Virginia, where the *Friendship* delivered its cargo, underwent repairs, and loaded up new cargo to take back to Great Britain. John had an older brother, William, who had moved to America some years before and worked as a tailor in Fredericksburg, Virginia. He probably stayed with his brother that summer.

It took five to six weeks to sail from Great Britain to America. The trip to America took longer than the trip home because of the Gulf Stream (not named as such in the eighteenth century) flowing to the east. By 1764 when he turned seventeen, John had crossed the Atlantic on the *Friendship* eight times. When hard economic times forced the owner to sell his ship, he released John from the second half of his seven-year apprenticeship. John accepted a job as a third mate, the fourth in command, aboard a slave ship that transported Africans to the Caribbean. Sailors called slave ships "black birders." John would go on to serve as the first mate of another slaver.

John Paul sailed the middle passage, the key leg of the slave trade. Traders chained African slaves to planks in the hold, the cargo area at the bottom of the ship, packing them close together. Each morning, the crew would weed out the slaves who had died the night before, carry them up to the main deck, and throw the bodies into the ocean. Slave traders factored in the number of slaves they could lose and still make a profit. Slave ships were said to project such a terrible odor from the filth and death that other ships did not want to sail too close.

There is no record of Paul's feelings about this period of his life, but three years after accepting the third mate's position, he had apparently had enough. He asked to be paid off after a voyage from Africa to Jamaica, which means he quit without waiting to get back to Scotland. The slave trade was controversial and could have harmed Paul's reputation, which he cared about very much. The slave trade was also the refuge of many scoundrels and thieves, and he may have quit after being cheated in some way.

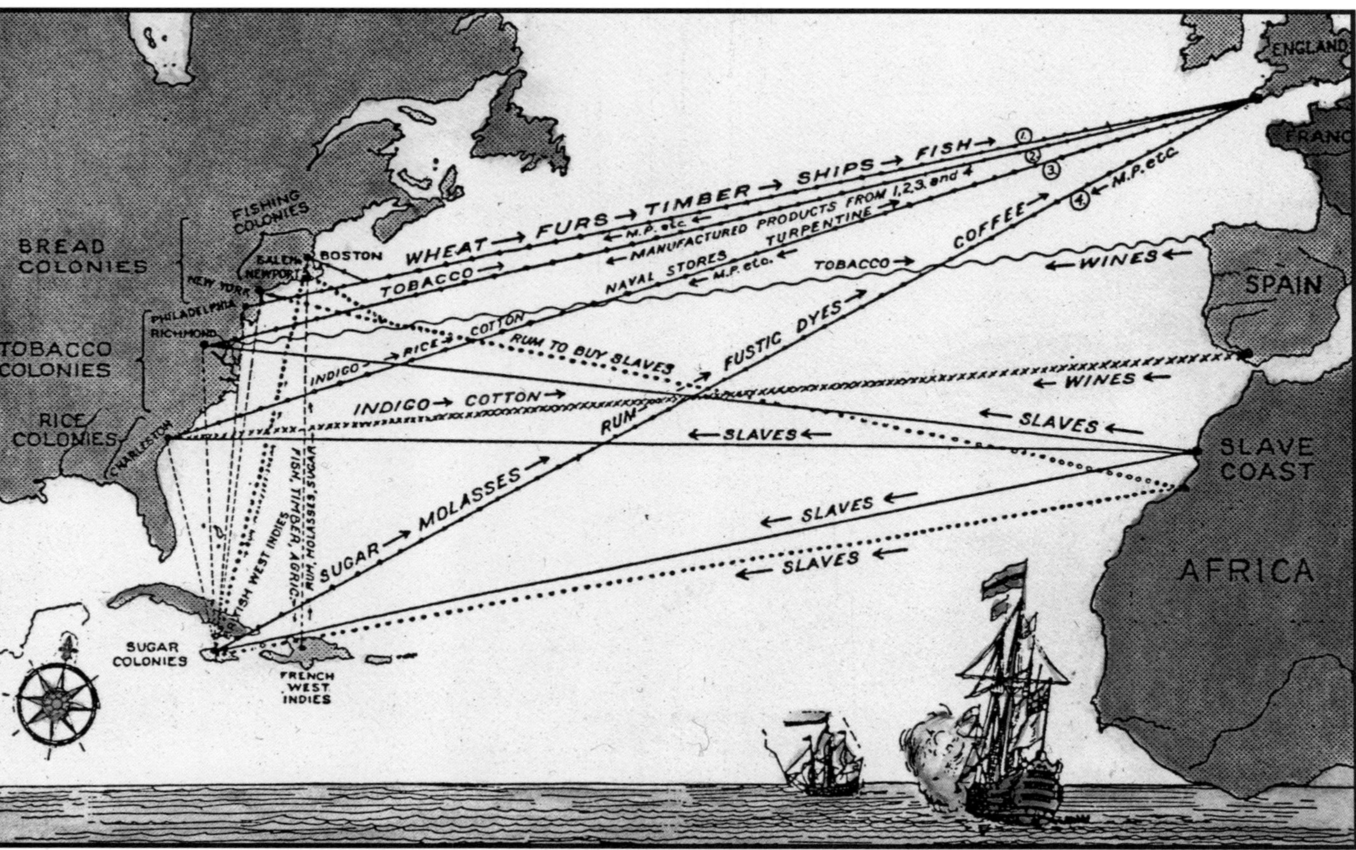

The slave trade in the seventeenth and eighteenth centuries was part of the triangular trade between Britain, its American colonies, and Africa. (Courtesy of the Granger Collection.)

The brutal Atlantic slave trade originated as a result of a labor shortage in the New World. The first slaves used were Native Americans, but they were not numerous enough, and European cruelty and diseases had decimated their numbers. The importing of slaves to Britain's North American colonies began in 1619 and continued into the nineteenth century. (Library of Congress)

Paul found himself unemployed in Kingston, Jamaica. The captain of a small ship, called a brig, offered him free passage back to Scotland. On the voyage back, both the captain and the first mate died of an unknown disease they had apparently picked up in Jamaica. Paul was the only one on board who could navigate, and he managed to safely bring the aptly named *John* home. The owners of the ship rewarded the twenty-one-year-old mariner with his first command. In only eight years, Paul had gone from apprentice, effectively a servant, to being the master of his own vessel.

Paul was a good captain, but not an easy one to work for. He demanded quality from his men. Sailors were often of two minds about a tough captain. They appreciated a skipper who seemed to know what hc was doing and mistrusted one who was too easy going or sloppy. But an overly strict captain could burden a ship with unnecessary rules and extra work. While Paul does not seem to have been a brutal captain, he apparently possessed a fussy and self-centered manner that made unnecessary enemies. This was a fault he would never outgrow, and which would later hurt his career.

Paul clashed with sailors he thought challenged his authority. On his second voyage from Scotland as a captain, the *John* had a carpenter's mate named Mungo Maxwell. Maxwell was from a prominent family in Kirkcudbright, the *John's* home port, not far from where Paul grew up. Maxwell was arrogant and cocky and did not want to take orders from the son of a gardener. Paul ordered Maxwell flogged as punishment.

Sailors were used to such seemingly drastic punishments, at least in the merchant navy. A shipboard thief, for example, might be flogged. (A thief on land, however, might be hanged.) But to flog a sailor for a bad attitude was unusual. It was not unheard of for a merchant sailor, after a flogging, to sue the captain for brutality when the ship reached port.

Maxwell did just this when the *John* reached Tobago. An admiralty court, charged with handling naval matters, was in session at the time. A judge examined Maxwell's back and found his wounds to be "neither mortal nor dangerous," quickly vindicating Paul. He also found that Maxwell's conduct and general incompetence had earned him the punishment. Maxwell quit the *John,* and sailed home to Scotland on another ship. Paul finished his business, picked up a return cargo, and then also returned to Scotland. Normally, the story would end there.

However, when the ship carrying Maxwell reached Scotland before the *John* arrived, it was discovered that Maxwell had died on the return voyage. His powerful family had Paul arrested and thrown in jail when he arrived in Scotland. The charge declared that Maxwell was "most unmercifully, by the said John Paul, with a great cudgel or batton, bled, bruised and wounded upon his back and other parts of his body, and of which wounds he soon afterward died."

Paul was allowed to bail himself out and to collect

evidence of his innocence. Most importantly, he obtained a statement from the captain of Maxwell's return ship that Maxwell had seemed in perfect health when he boarded and later caught a fever and died at sea. Records from Tobago showed that Paul had already been cleared by a court of abusing Maxwell. The Scottish courts dismissed the charge.

Still, the arrest infuriated Paul. He was particularly upset that Lord Craik, on whose estate he had grown up, sided with the Maxwells. He later wrote his mother that Craik's "ungracious conduct to me before I left Scotland I have not yet been able to get the better of." Paul was probably correct in believing he had been the victim of aristocratic arrogance. But Paul always brooded over insults, real or imagined. He was an ambitious man who guarded his honor with too much sensitivity and never realized that brooding was a self-destructive trait.

Paul, looking for social connections to help him in future conflicts, became a Freemason. The Masons were a hybrid of a social club, an educational organization, and a center for philosophy. Membership was also a way to network with others in order to advance in society. The Masons had started out as an aristocratic group. By the time Jones joined in November 1770, Masonry had become a means of upward social mobility for the middle class, which included sea captains. Masons were secretive about their organization and had a system of degrees of participation. Members were inducted through a process that included ritual exploration of metaphysical issues. Paul would remain a Mason all of his life.

While he was becoming a Mason and clearing himself of the Maxwell charges, the owners of the *John* sold their ship. They gave their twenty-four-year-old captain an excellent recommendation, writing that "he approved himself every way qualified." Paul soon obtained command

John Paul Jones was one of many influential American Revolution-era Freemasons, including the country's first president, George Washington, and first Supreme Court chief justice, John Marshall. (Library of Congress)

of a larger ship, the *Betsy,* based in London. Its owners promised a share of the profits from each voyage.

London was then the largest city in the western world, with a population of nearly one million. London was also one of the most unsanitary cities in the world. Residents dumped raw sewage into the streets, and overhead smog from the early beginnings of the Industrial Revolution left heavy layers of soot on everything exposed, often blocking out the sun. Among the sights a newcomer to London would see was the gallows at Wapping, at a place called Executioner's Dock, where pirates were hanged at low tide and their bodies left to rot for several days. There were efforts underway to improve London. The government was paving streets with stones, removing sewage ditches, and building a few parks.

Society, however, was becoming even more stratified, and the new wealth earned in business and professions such as law began to openly compete with the old landed aristocracy for social status. The more the aristocracy lost out financially, the more they pushed back against the rising middle class socially. The ambitious young Paul encountered both subtle and open arrogance in his dealings with Royal Navy officers, who were convinced that merchant officers, even merchant captains, were their social inferiors. Merchant ship masters might become rich, but they would not be accepted by the "real" aristocrats. Breeding always won out. Naval officers, most of whom came from the upper class, would be

Eighteenth-century London, spanning the Thames River, was a booming port and intriguing city for a young, ambitious sailor such as John Paul Jones. (Library of Congress)

friendly and affable, as any other "gentleman" would, but not familiar.

Paul, for his part, was not easy to befriend, or to be cordial toward. He remained insecure, perhaps trying a bit too hard to please. He bristled at any hint of condescension. This sensitivity extended to his subordinates and eventually led to the most critical incident of his early career.

About a year after taking command of the *Betsy,* Paul found himself in the West Indies. The trip had already been delayed during the summer of 1773 while the ship underwent extensive repairs in Ireland. Paul was ill during this period. However, he made it to Tobago just before Christmas, where he took on some new crewmen. Among them was a fellow known to history, through Paul's letters, as "the Ringleader." Many years later, Paul described this man as "a prodigious brute of thrice [my] strength . . . [who] neglected and even refused his duty with much insolence."

Most merchant ship mutinies of the period started over money and this one was no different. Paul had little extra cash, due to repairs and some ruined cargo, and instead of following his normal procedure of advancing wages to his crew, he decided to invest the money in a new cargo. The men would be paid when they got back to London. The Ringleader grumbled the loudest about this, but Paul ignored him and went ashore to attend to business.

On return to the ship, Paul found that the Ringleader was stirring up the crew and threatening to steal the ship's launch—the small boat carried on a ship. As Paul later wrote, the "brute" confronted him with "the grossest abuse that vulgarism could dictate." Paul tried to compromise by offering the Ringleader some clothing from the ship's extra supplies. Apparently, this was a mistake. The Ringleader became enraged at being offered spare clothing instead of money and "swore with horrid imprecations that he would take away the boat by force."

Paul briefly retreated to his cabin. Later, in a letter to Benjamin Franklin that serves as the only description of the incident, Paul claimed that he intended to grab a stick but

The story of John Paul's encounter with the Ringleader, as well as rumors of his generally unorthodox treatment of fellow sailors, would follow him throughout his life. (Courtesy of the Granger Collection.)

by chance his sword was lying on the table, so he grabbed that instead. He also claimed he only intended to make a show of force, but that the Ringleader intended to fight, grabbed an unnamed "bludgeon," and advanced on him.

Paul found himself isolated on deck, his officers nowhere to be seen, with his crew clearly favoring the Ringleader. The man advanced toward Paul, who backed up. Seconds later, Paul felt his heel strike the edge of a hatchway to the decks below. Further retreat and he would fall down the stairs. As Paul described it, he suddenly stopped, the Ringleader lunged forward, only to be impaled and killed by Paul's sword. Paul, though he would have been justified to stab the man coming to injure or kill him, claimed the death was an accident.

Paul turned himself in to the local authorities, and while he was not arrested, he understood he would have to face legal proceedings of some kind. Having been through something similar, but less serious, with the Mungo Maxwell affair, Paul had confidence that the courts would clear him. Admiralty courts usually backed the authority of a captain. However, the local admiralty court was not in session, which meant he might have to face a jury trial for murder in an ordinary court, with jurors who might be friends of the Ringleader, a local man. Paul, possibly encouraged by his business partner, decided to flee and caught a ship to North America. His plan was to lay low until his partner sent him enough money to return to face a trial before a sympathetic admiralty court.

The money would never come. Adding "Jones" to his given name of John Paul, he spent the next year and a half in Fredericksburg, Virginia. His older brother William had died, but John Paul Jones liked the area and stayed. No evidence exists as to what he did during this period, which ended with the summer of 1775. He may have simply lived off the funds he brought from Tobago.

Jones wrote only to the famous Benjamin Franklin about the incident with the Ringleader when he thought Franklin had heard of it from other sources. He insisted he had acted in self-defense. But the fact that he seems never to have told anyone else about the incident, and that he only told Franklin when he thought it was already known, indicated he was sensitive about it. He might have realized that his own low tolerance for insolence and his quick temper had contributed to the tragedy.

Three

War at Sea

Jones soon discovered that Americans were a seafaring people. The year was 1775, and war against the greatest naval power in the world lay on the horizon. Many wondered how the upstart colonies could hope to contend with the British fleet. But there was talent and experience available. In late 1775, an informant identified only as B. P. wrote the British sub-cabinet minister in charge of America about the quality of the colonial ship captains: "Many of the Captains of these vessels, in the last war [the French and Indian War, in which the American colonies fought with Britain against France], proved their intrepidity to the world. . . . [The Americans would be no] contemptible enemy at sea."

It is natural that many of the European settlers in North America were oriented to the sea. They or their

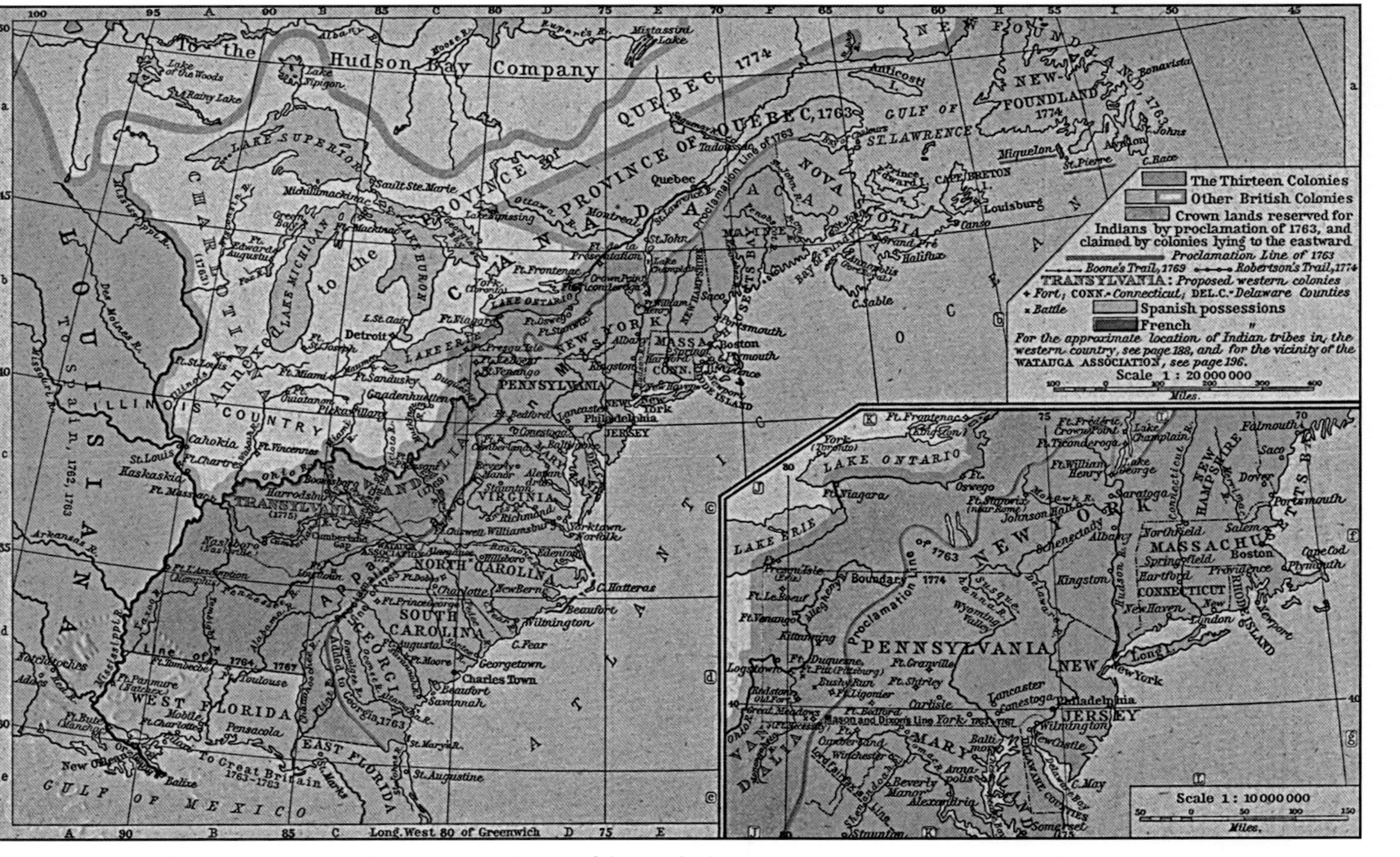

Britain's colonial possessions in North America on the eve of the revolution. (Courtesy of the Perry-Castañeda Library Map Collection, University of Texas, Austin.)

ancestors had sailed the Atlantic Ocean to reach America, and many made their living sailing back and forth or by sending agricultural products to, and buying supplies from, Great Britain. Sailing up and down the coast was the main means of communication and trade between the colonies. Even much of the heavier traffic inland was waterborne, using the many rivers that flowed down from the eastern mountains.

The colonists took a while getting to know the land and learning how to use the resources of the forest. In the beginning, the heavy forests of North America overwhelmed the landscape. It was said a squirrel could

A prosperous village in early colonial America. (Library of Congress)

travel from Maine to Georgia without ever having to leave a tree. Because the colonists settled near the Atlantic, most transportation involved sailing along the coastline. Fish was a major source of food, and soon a fishing industry thrived.

The primary motivation for shipbuilding, however, was trade. The economies of the colonies and European nations depended upon the moving of raw products from North America to Europe and the sending of finished and manufactured goods back. Most of this commercial traffic took place on so-called "tall" ships, which were made of wood. The plentiful forests of North America provided the lumber needed to build the ships. Tall trees proved particularly valuable because they could easily be turned into masts for the oceangoing vessels. American wood resources became so important to Britain that their loss as a result of the American Revolution was one of the many motivating factors that sped up the early development of the Industrial Revolution in Britain.

Shipbuilders were among the earliest settlers in Virginia and Massachusetts. As Massachusetts became more active in shipbuilding, its colonial government provided tax incentives to shipbuilders. Vessels were not taxed until they were launched, for example. The colony also appointed quality-control inspectors, who were supposed to ensure that only sound timber was used. Unfortunately, this quality control did not last. Particularly during the period just before and during the American Revolution, American shipbuilders frequently rushed construction, producing slipshod work with wood not given enough time to age properly. American ships often did not last as long as those built in Britain and in Europe.

Great Britain passed navigation acts in the mid-1600s, designed to protect the British shipping industry from competition from the other major maritime powers, primarily France, Spain, and the Netherlands. These acts required all trade within the British Empire to be shipped on British or American ships. This was a boon to the American shipbuilding industry, which spread south from New England, through New York, to Philadelphia. By the time of the American Revolution, Philadelphia was the largest shipbuilding center in the American colonies. The southern colonies tended to concentrate on smaller vessels, suitable for use in the sandbar-laced waters off Virginia and the Carolinas.

Shipbuilding was a low-tech activity, with virtually all the work done with hand tools. Prefabricated sections, welded together at the shipyard, wouldn't exist for two centuries. The work began with selecting the wood. Builders used oak, a strong and durable wood, for the hull. Pine worked best for the masts and spars, the crosspieces securing and stretching out the sails. Pine was flexible and could handle the stress the mast would be subjected to during travel.

Gangs of workmen would be sent into the forest to cut the timber and bring it to the shipyard. Shipbuilders preferred to collect wood during the winter when the trees had less sap in them and could season in less time. They also preferred trees near streams, though this resource would soon be exhausted. The workmen could float the logs down the stream to the yard. Otherwise, teams of oxen had to drag them.

At the yard, the logs would be dragged across a deep pit for conversion into boards. Two men, one in the pit and one above, slowly cut the logs into planks. This process would be substantially improved later with the development of sawmills.

While the plans were being prepared, shipwrights (best described as a cross between naval architects and carpenters) would prepare the area where they would build the ship. Men would place posts to mark the back and side of the ship-to-be. Shipwrights would usually work from experience, but some would draw up work plans.

When the planks were ready, the framework for the vessel was constructed starting amidships (in the middle) and working fore and aft—to the front and to the back. Once the vertical planks were in place, the builders fastened horizontal planks to the inside of the ship with long trunnels, or wooden nails, placed in holes already drilled. Thousands of trunnels were used. The inside of the hull briefly took on the appearance of an inside-out porcupine before the ends of the wooden nails were trimmed off. Iron fastenings were available, but they were expensive and tended to corrode from the seawater and the tannic acid of the oak planks. Once the planks

This busy shipyard in eighteenth-century New England gives a sense of some of the many stages involved in the shipbuilding process. (Courtesy of the Granger Collection.)

were in place, the caulkers would go to work. They used a substance called oakum—hemp treated with tar—to seal the seams of the vessel, pounding it into place. Sealing was never perfect, and ships usually had some system for pumping out water. Finally, the builders installed the decks of the ship.

When a new ship was launched—even in Massachusetts, at the height of power of the stern Puritans—the owner would christen it. In the ceremony someone would call out the name the ship had been given and then break a bottle of rum over the front edge of the ship. The ship-launching ceremony remains virtually unchanged to this day. The ship was then taken to a nearby wharf where the final details were completed. The average time for construction of a fully masted, rigged, and fitted ship was about one year.

American shipyards could build large ships, but the focus was on durability, speed, and maneuverability. Americans preferred to build schooners rather than larger, square-rigged ships. The sails of a schooner run parallel to the bow, while the square rigged sails lay perpendicular.

American ships became popular in the eighteenth century more for their inexpensive cost than for their good design. American-built ships could be as much as 50 percent cheaper, relative to weight, than those built elsewhere. Labor cost more in the colonies, but this was more than offset by low material costs. American ships had a reputation for using poor-quality materials, and some complained that the boats rotted faster than others. This is likely due to poor selection of wood, as well as failure to properly season it. Ideally, once the frame of a wooden ship was assembled, it should be allowed to sit for a year. This was not economically feasible in small American shipyards. Sometimes the wood in American ships had only aged for the time it took to get the wood to the shipyard.

American shipyards built a lot of ships for the British merchant service but only four large ships for the Royal Navy. The quality of the workmanship did not meet the navy's standards. Warships had to carry a heavy load of artillery, and the British naval officials worried that

American-built ships would not stand the weight of their guns. American shipwrights did, however, have the chance to observe warship construction from the extensive repair work done on Royal Navy vessels in American yards. They were also acquainted with warship design.

Jones came to the colonies on the eve of the American Revolution, the war in which he would gain the fame he so desired. The break with Great Britain had been a long time coming and was driven by an assortment of economic, social, and religious causes. The result being that by the summer of 1775, the rift had grown too wide to repair. As Benjamin Franklin wrote to a British acquaintance in February 1779, as Jones was preparing for his greatest battle: "The Truth is we have no kind of Faith in your Government."

The specific chain of events that led to the revolution might be said to have begun on July 3, 1754, when a young American colonial officer surrendered his band of militia to a force of French soldiers. During the surrender, the militia officer signed a document, written in French, which he thought stated that his men had killed a French officer in another incident a few months before. The document actually stated that the French officer had been assassinated, a far more serious charge. When he headed back to Virginia, young George Washington had no idea he had touched off a war between Great Britain and its longtime enemy France.

The roots of the war were in Europe, where national and diplomatic rivalries, excessively complex systems of alliance and diplomatic maneuvers, and the Prussian invasion of Saxony led to the start of war. The conflict soon spread to other areas of the world. The war outside of America became known as the Seven Years War. Inside America, it took the name of the French and Indian War, because various tribes fought on both sides.

For several years, the war in America did not go well for the British and their colonists. French and Indian forces pushed the frontier of British settlement back 150 miles. The British made the job harder for themselves by the way they initially conducted the war. Their overall strategy was good, but tactically they tried to fight the war as if they were fighting on the relatively open fields of Europe rather than the heavily forested terrain of North America. Conventional tactics did not work very well against the unconventional methods the French learned from their Indian allies.

The British also refused to take any advice from the colonial military and political leadership. Colonial troops were constantly reminded of their second-class status. Colonial officers, of whatever rank, had to take orders from any British officer, no matter how low he ranked. Regular British officers received command assignments taken from colonial officers. There was also a tendency to appoint regular officers due to political connections, not ability.

The British paid a price for their arrogance. The war went against them for almost four years. Things began to change in December of 1756 when William Pitt,

This late-nineteenth-century wood engraving shows the Marquis de Montcalm, commander of the French forces in North America during the French and Indian War, attempting to stop Native-American warriors from attacking British soldiers and civilians as they leave Fort William Henry near Lake George in New York. (Library of Congress)

formerly a major voice in opposition to the conduct of the war, was appointed to the British cabinet post of what was then called secretary of state for the Southern Department. From this position, he effectively ran the war in America and Europe.

Pitt took a more creative and active approach to running the war. He picked his commanders in America on the basis of ability, even if this meant picking colonials over British regulars. Pitt also spent heavily without regard to the effect on the British economy and treasury.

Great Britain eventually won the war in 1763, but by then the country was nearly broke. This dire fiscal situation led to a series of bad decisions, which in turn led to other things going wrong. In October 1761, William

Pitt left the cabinet—but retained his seat in the British Parliament. The next step into the abyss came from fighting against various Indian groups, generally known as Pontiac's War or Pontiac's Rebellion, after the most prominent Indian leader involved. General Jeffrey Amherst, the British army commander in North America, spent nearly a year in subduing the Indians.

King George III considered the Native Americans to be his subjects and believed that a good king had to look after his subjects. His government revised Amherst's harsh policy of subjugation of the Native Americans to one of pacification. One of the measures adopted was a halt in western expansion. This was likely a temporary measure; the British were not going to give up the wealth that could be gained by the western expansion they had fought a long war against the French to achieve.

The halt on expansion irritated the colonials, who argued that the Native Americans and the settlers could learn to get along on their own. The prohibition thwarted the dreams of many ambitious colonists, such as George Washington, who longed to expand their holdings over the eastern mountain range.

Money was the primary motivator of British policy toward the American colonies in the period after the end of fighting with the French. British national debt had more than doubled during the war. Political realities made it almost impossible for the government to raise taxes enough in Britain to pay for colonial defense and the debt accumulated in the war. British political leaders made what they thought was not only the most politically viable choice but also one they considered most fair. The colonies would have to pay for their own defense through taxes. Levying taxes in the colonies would also allow the mother country to have more control over the independent-minded colonies. The colonies could not reasonably object to a slight increase in their tax burden, the British thought. Americans would still have less than five percent of the tax burden of residents of Britain. They had no right to object to what the British government considered a restoration of the proper relationship with Britain.

In 1763, the British parliament passed a measure designed to increase and regulate enforcement of existing tariffs. This annoyed the colonials, and in combination with a new import duty on sugar passed the next year, provoked peaceful protest. However, real problems began in 1765, with the passage of the Stamp Act. British prime minister George Grenville thought that this act requiring revenue stamps on official documents and publications would not be controversial. He was wrong. The targets of the tax included lawyers, ministers, ship owners, academics, printers, and publishers. These were the very people most likely to protest, and to know how to protest effectively.

Colonists were so incensed by the Stamp Act that they convened a Stamp Act Congress that fall, gathering in New York City to protest the constitutionality of the act. Their contention was that no free man could be taxed without his consent, a consent that colonists could not possibly give since they were not represented in the English Parliament.

Grenville, the other British ministers, and the king all misread the effect these taxes would have on the Americans. Americans had become accustomed to being treated as equals to Britain. The British government ignored the lessons of William Pitt, who had known how to get American cooperation in the war against the French—by treating them as partners.

Furthermore, the French threat, which might have justified increased taxes to influential Americans, was gone. It seemed to many Americans that now that the British no longer needed their help, they were determined to return the colonists to subject status. The American colonists expected to be treated as more than second-class citizens.

The famous "no taxation without representation" cry arose during this period, but probably did not have the importance credited to it by popular history. In truth, the British Parliament was not truly representative of the people living in Britain, either. The government was corrupted by "rotten boroughs," in which wealthy aristocrats represented their own interests and employed various other methods that made sure Parliament spoke only for a small segment of British society. In reality, many in the colonies wanted to be self-governing. Many of the new leaders of the movement against Great Britain did not want parliamentary representation. They wanted their own government and control of their own affairs without interference from across the Atlantic Ocean.

The outcry against the Stamp Act was so loud and sometimes violent that it was repealed after a few months, primarily due to William Pitt's efforts in Parliament. (Grenville recommended using British troops to enforce the act.) But this did not end the conflict. The next eight years became a duel of wills between the colonists and the British government, under several prime ministers. The result might have been different had the British not insisted on firm control over the colonies or had they looked more at the economic value of trade with the colonies than at the abstract urge to maintain total control. As time went on, the colonials reached the point of no return when its leaders considered every British move, mild as many were by historical standards, as an attempt to establish tyranny. In short, by 1775, trust was gone and the differences were irreconcilable.

By 1773, the British had eliminated all taxes on the colonies except for a tax on tea. George III wanted one tax kept as a symbol of the British right to tax the colonies. The levy was so low that taxed tea was actually cheaper than smuggled tea, but the symbolism was all that mattered at this point. On the night of December 16, 1773, a mob overran three British ships loaded with tea and dumped the cargo into Boston Harbor. At the time, the average laborer made a dollar a day. The Bostonians threw $90,000 worth of tea into the harbor.

Radicals in America, such as Samuel Adams, were

Angry colonists in Boston burn a copy of the Stamp Act during a riot in August 1765. (Library of Congress)

delighted, and moderates appalled. These events outraged the British government, which proceeded to overreact—despite the protests of some moderates in Parliament—uniting the American moderates and radicals by their rash response. The British closed Boston Harbor, limiting the import of food into the colony and curtailing the power of the Massachusetts colonial government. Local officials were to be appointed in London; town meetings, the core of self-government in Massachusetts, were limited to one per year.

The British strengthened the law requiring locals to quarter British troops; British troops could be permanently stationed in Massachusetts. Quartering troops in private homes was a last resort. The real purpose of the law was to force the colonies to pay for building barracks for the troops in order to get them out of their homes.

The British government agreed to end all taxes on America if the colonial governments would voluntarily contribute to the cost of defending the empire, primarily against France and Spain. Similar arrangements had proven important in turning the tide during the French

In one of the most famous political protests in American history, approximately sixty Bostonians, known as the Sons of Liberty, destroyed 342 crates of tea during what came to be known as the Boston Tea Party. When they were finished, the colonists took off their shoes, swept and tidied the decks, and made the first mate of each tea ship attest that only the tea had been destroyed. (Library of Congress)

Americans throwing the Cargoes of the Tea Ships into the River, at Boston

and Indian War. This might have worked but for continuing efforts to punish Massachusetts. On April 12, 1775, British general Thomas Gage declared all residents of Massachusetts to be traitors, but offered them all pardons except for Samuel Adams and John Hancock, whom he accurately considered the two most troublesome leaders. Paul Revere's first ride, on April 16, served to warn these men to flee from Lexington before British soldiers arrived.

During his second and most famous ride, on April 18, Revere warned all colonists that British troops were headed to Concord by way of Lexington to seize arms secretly gathered by local patriot militia groups. Not long after dawn on April 19, 1775, about seventy untrained members of the Massachusetts militia confronted several hundred British regulars on Lexington Green. The British commander ordered the militia to disperse. The colonial commander told them to stay. Normally, the British would have just ignored the militia and marched around them. But this time the sides continued to glower at each other until some shots, from an unknown source, rang out. The British soldiers fired and then disobeyed orders to surround the colonials without shooting, continuing with the attack. A bayonet charge followed, which finally dispersed the colonials. Eight militia men died, ten were wounded. One British soldier suffered a slight wound.

Before the day was over, the two sides had fought again at Concord Bridge in a running battle, with the

Americans sniping from cover as the British marched back to Boston. The British lost about one hundred men, the Americans about half that. As battles go, this was not a significant number of casualties, but April 19, 1775, was one of the most influential days in modern history. The American war for independence from Great Britain had begun.

Four

The Continental Navy

While he lived in Fredericksburg, Virginia, in the years just before the Revolutionary War began, Jones probably lived off the money he brought with him when he fled Tobago. He joined the local Masonic lodge in Fredericksburg and apparently spent some time studying, trying to improve his general knowledge, as would befit a gentleman of the eighteenth century. One commentator of the period, who had worked as a tutor to the sons of Virginia gentry, wrote, "Any young gentleman traveling through Virginia was presumed to be acquainted with dancing, boxing, card and fiddle-playing and the use of the small sword."

Jones became a believer in the increasingly popular philosophy of what came to be called the Enlightenment. The core of this philosophy was a faith in reason and the social idea that merit, not birth, should determine how high a person rose in society.

Gentlemen also prided themselves on classical learning, and Jones worked hard to improve his education. One of his midshipmen during the Revolutionary War—a junior officer undergoing shipboard training—later wrote, "The learning he obtained . . . from the age of nine years, was from close application to books, of which he was remarkably fond." Jones became noted for letters and reports that were much better written than those of most sea captains. He particularly liked Shakespeare's tragedy *Othello,* once including in a letter the line: "I should have found within my soul one drop of patience." Shakespeare's original is virtually the same.

Othello is a noble figure, but one continually feeling disappointed and betrayed and with a core of paranoia. His enemy, Iago, uses this paranoia to destroy Othello. Jones's use of the quote seems to show a rare piece of self-knowledge, at least recognizing that he could not have things his way all the time and that he might not always see the total perspective.

Early in the fall of 1775, Jones traveled to Philadelphia to offer his services to revolutionary leadership. He never recorded his reasons for enlisting. One can speculate that he saw a chance to support his new society and its opportunities for advancement, and to satisfy his desire for fame. He possessed valuable qualities and experience to offer the fledgling government. He had commanded a ship and would know how to get a warship

Philadelphia, the most populous city north of Mexico City during the Revolutionary era, was a major center of the independence movement, largely due to efforts made by one of its most prominent citizens, Benjamin Franklin. (Library of Congress)

where it was needed and how to lead it in battle. His first ship had been armed—during the French and Indian War—so he had some experience with a semi-war ship. The only problem was that there was no navy for him to join.

Philadelphia was the capital of the thirteen colonies. It was also the center for mobilization, outside of the soldiers directly facing the British in Boston. Troops drilled in the streets, including units of Quakers—officially a pacifist religion. Cannons and barrels of gunpowder were piled high on the green behind the State House. The colonies had no gunpowder factories; it had to be smuggled past the blockade the British were already putting around the harbors. A Dutch ship, anchored at the city dock on the Delaware River, was filled with

49,000 pounds of gunpowder—a literal powder keg.

Jones found himself in a city seemingly as much concerned with politics as with preparing for war. Politics never ends even when war begins. This was especially true here, in a revolution that would always maintain some characteristics of a civil war. Though the conviction that it was time to be separate from Great Britain was growing, most colonists still considered themselves loyal Englishmen who were being forced to fight for their rights as such. They also considered themselves to be citizens of thirteen sovereignties, not citizens of a unified country. Military planning had to take these political realities into account. Spending had to be dispersed to allow as many areas as possible to participate, regardless of military necessity.

The leaders of the colonies had agreed to send representatives to a Continental Congress to coordinate the resistance to Britain. The first Continental Congress had little actual power. It met in 1774 to decide how to react to the British closure of Boston Harbor. The second Continental Congress met the next year and discussed the need for a land army. The New England militia, including the Massachusetts units that had taken part in the fighting at Lexington and Concord, had organized the troops besieging the British in Boston. The Congress decided to organize a Continental army from all the colonies to fight the mighty British forces. George Washington, now a successful northern Virginia plantation owner, was given command of this new army.

An army was one thing, but creating a navy proved more difficult and raised serious political issues. Independent nations had navies, and the Congress had not yet decided whether they wanted independence. Furthermore, the task of trying to match the Royal Navy, the largest and most powerful navy in the world, was clearly an impossible goal. The Congress debated whether the best use of resources would be to focus on building an army. Samuel Chase, a delegate from Maryland, said the talk of building a navy was "the maddest idea in the world." John Adams claimed that building an American navy "represented the most wild, visionary, mad project that has ever been imagined."

As the Congress weighed options, colonists began to act. Some of the colonies organized their own navies and ordered the building of their own ships, outfitting privateers to attack British commerce. Privateers are vessels fitted out by private owners but licensed by the government to attack enemy commerce. Congress began to license privateers, although it was pointed out that the only difference between the privateer and a pirate was the "letter of marque," government authorization to wage war on commerce.

George Washington also had his own navy to complement the Continental army. Composed of smaller New England-built ships that were used to harass British commerce and smaller warships, one of Washington's ships even managed to seize a British cargo vessel with 2,000 muskets and ammunition.

One big question remained when Jones got to Philadelphia: Would Congress authorize the building of a national navy? On October 5, 1775, the Rhode Island delegation introduced a resolution calling for "building at the Continental expense a fleet of sufficient force, for the protection of these colonies, and for employing them in such a manner and places as will effectively annoy our enemies." About this time, a report of two unescorted British merchant ships on the way to America arrived, motivating Congress to action. They wanted to seize these ships.

Building a navy would take time and money. Congress allocated almost $900,000 for the construction of thirteen frigates. In the meantime, they bought and borrowed a collection of merchant ships to convert to warships.

A navy also needed experienced officers. Some member of Congress turned to friends and family members. Stephen Hopkins, the chairman of the Congressional naval committee, got his brother Esek the job of commanding the fleet. Dudley Saltonstall, brother-in-law of committee member Silas Deane, became captain of the *Alfred,* which, with its thirty guns, was the largest of the American ships.

Though he later complained about this method of picking officers, Jones was offered command of a ship called the *Providence* through his connections to Joseph Hewes, a North Carolina merchant and a member of the same naval committee. Jones had some concerns about taking command of this ship. *Providence* was a sloop, a ship with one large mast in the center and a gigantic sail running parallel to the deck. Sloops could be difficult to handle. Jones finally decided to decline this command—a decision he later regretted—and asked for a position as second in command of a larger but square-rigged vessel—one on which the sails were perpendicular to the bow. In December 1775, the Continental Navy commissioned John Paul Jones as a first lieutenant. He became the first person to raise an American flag over a navy vessel when he hoisted the flag over his first assignment, the *Alfred.* The flag he raised was a hybrid of the colonial and the British. It had thirteen stripes representing the colonies, but the British flag remained in the part now occupied by the fifty stars.

Jones, the executive officer, fitted out the ship for sea

The Grand Union flag, which Jones raised on the Alfred *on December 3, 1775.*

and combat. He did an effective job, including training the gun crews, but discovered at least one major problem with his ship: it was "crank." This meant that in a stiff breeze it might tip over on one side. At the very least, the gun ports on that side would have to be shut and could not be used in battle. If the gun-port shutters were left open, the ship might sink.

A five-ship fleet, commanded by Esek Hopkins, with Jones onboard the *Alfred,* finally moved into the Atlantic Ocean in February 1776, when the ice blocking the Delaware River thawed. Hopkins was under orders to destroy some British ships harassing the area of the Chesapeake Bay, then go to North Carolina, and finally to Rhode Island. However, before effective ship-to-ship communications, commanders often treated naval orders like suggestions. Seizing on a loophole in his orders that allowed him to use his best judgment, Hopkins decided to head for the warm waters near Bermuda and try to capture some gunpowder. Four sailors had smallpox, which he considered an accident, justifying the alteration of his orders.

By the time Hopkins reached the warmer water two of the ships had got lost in a storm—they made it back to port later. The remaining American vessels anchored off an old pirates' lair near Bermuda. They captured two British schooners and learned that Bermuda did have a sizable stock of gunpowder. Bermuda was undefended, with most British troops just having left.

Hopkins planned to hide three hundred marines be-

Commodore Esek Hopkins, commander of the American fleet throughout the Revolutionary War.

low decks of the captured schooners and send them into the harbor of Nassau, the largest town, to take it by surprise. This was a good plan, but was poorly executed. Because Hopkins let his ships sail too close to town, rather than stay over the horizon, they were spotted and the element of surprise was lost. Jones later claimed that he then suggested an alternative. "It was I who developed the plan," he later wrote, but Hopkins did not mention him in his report written later. The plan called for using the marines in an attack on the easternmost of the two forts guarding the harbor.

The Continental Marines landed under fire—the first U.S. Marine landing in history—and captured the fort. Then, instead of heading directly for Nassau, they rested for the night, a costly delay. By the time the town was taken, the British governor had managed to load the gunpowder on a ship and send it to safety. The Americans did manage to capture over ninety artillery pieces, 16,000 cannonballs and shells, and twenty barrels of gunpowder. It was valuable weaponry, but this was not the smashing victory that had been possible.

On the way back with the weapons, Hopkins's squadron ran into a twenty-four-gun British warship, the *Glasgow*. Standard naval tactics called for the American ships to form a "line of battle"—to sail in a line past the British ship, firing in turn. The ideal tactic would have been to "cross the t"—to sail in front of the British frigate. Hitting the enemy in rapid succession would likely have resulted in a quick American victory. But the American ships fought one at a time, and the British fought them off. After about an hour of combat, the British captain decided he had pushed his luck far enough and retreated. Hopkins's ships pursued, but the *Glasgow* safely escaped.

Casualties were very low in this first formal American naval battle in history. The British losses included one killed, three wounded; the Americans suffered ten dead, fourteen wounded. Jones was proud of how well his men had performed. He wrote his patron .Joseph Hewes, "I formed an exercise and trained the men so well to the great guns on the *Alfred* that they went thro' the motions of broad sides and rounds as exactly as soldiers generally perform their manual exercise." The British casualties, however, were caused by Marine gunfire.

Apparently, there had been other problems with the operations. A letter exists from Jones's chief gunner apologizing for his behavior towards Jones. This letter, a rather formal way of communicating between shipmates, may have been forced from the gunner by Jones. Good officers should get along with their senior noncommissioned officers. Jones apparently also conflicted with his immediate boss, Captain Dudley Saltonstall. In a report to Hewes, Jones was likely referring to Saltonstall when he wrote, "It is certainly for the Intrest of the Service that a Cordial interchange of Civilities should subsist between Superiour and Inferiour officers—and therefore it is bad policy in Superiours to behave towards their inferiours indiscriminately as tho' they were of a lower Species."

There are no specific incidents reported between Jones and Saltonstall. Apparently Jones simply resented what he saw as arrogance in his captain's behavior. But one had to wonder whether the same problems existed between Jones and the chief gunner. Jones had his moments of perception about his own behavior, but he was never good at dealing with others.

Jones did, however, manage to part on good terms

with Saltonstall. After the captain of the *Providence* was court-martialed for stealing his ship's supplies and removed from command, the navy again offered Jones a command. This time he accepted.

A crew of seventy-three officers and men, including twenty-five marines, manned the *Providence* and its twelve cannons. Marines were stationed on naval ships to keep order among the crew and to serve as snipers during combat. They were sometimes used to disembark and seize shorelines, or to attack entrenched positions.

Providence headed out to sea under the command of John Paul Jones on August 26, 1776. Its orders were to perform general patrolling and to capture British merchant

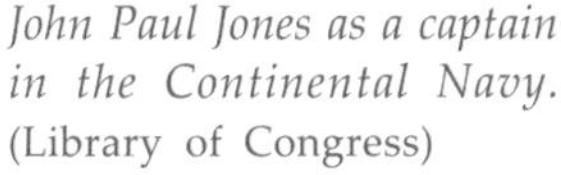

John Paul Jones as a captain in the Continental Navy. (Library of Congress)

vessels. After a week out at sea, lookouts reported spotting the masts of five ships just over the horizon. Jones's officers said they thought the largest was a sizable merchant ship. He thought this might be wrong but decided to go after the ships. When they got closer, the Americans discovered that the British ship was actually the frigate *Solebay,* armed twice as well as the *Providence.* Jones's ship was fast and maneuverable but not heavily armed. Now he was about to tangle with a far larger and stronger ship.

A good naval commander knows when not to fight. Jones ordered his ship to turn and flee. The British ship gave chase. Normally the *Providence* could quickly outpace the *Solebay*. The American ship could sail closer to the wind (not directly into a wind blowing from the front, but at less steep an angle), but this day the sea ran perpendicular to the paths of both ships, substantially slowing the *Providence.* The British ship gained slowly. As the British got closer, Jones and his crew could clearly see them getting ready to fire.

Jones, exhibiting the fearlessness that would make him famous, raised the American flag and ordered his guns to be ready to fire. The British captain also raised the American flag and had one of his guns fire a signal that the ship was friendly. Under the customs of the time such a ruse was acceptable—unless it was used to lure an enemy onto the rocks. Disguising oneself as the enemy is even legal under modern rules, along as one does not open fire under false colors or in a false uniform.

Jones was not fooled. He knew the American navy had no frigates of that size. He prepared his own surprise. The *Providence* suddenly spun around and, with a change of sail, shot across the bow of the *Solebay.* Sailing in the same direction of the wind, the *Providence* was nearly out of cannon range by the time the British could turn around, safely escaping. This was the most dramatic event of this first voyage, but it was a useful cruise. Jones and his crew captured or sank sixteen British merchant ships and sent six ships to American ports as prizes to be sold and the profits given to the crew.

Boarding a ship to capture it was preferable to sinking it. A captured ship could be sold for prize money, some of which the commander would distribute among the crew. A ship that was sunk held no value to anyone. Boarding could be more dangerous, however, and sometimes American crews would shy away from danger.

A month later, Jones found himself back on the *Alfred,* but this time Congress had promoted him to captain. Jones now commanded a small fleet, including the *Providence;* he was ordered to try to rescue American sailors taken prisoner by the British, who were using them as slave laborers in Nova Scotia coal mines. By the time he reached Nova Scotia though, the prisoners had managed their own form of escape by agreeing to enlist in the British navy.

As the *Alfred* was headed out to sea, the lookout spotted a mast on Naushon Island, a small island just off Cape Cod, Massachusetts, that had once been a haven for pirates. Jones sent some marines to investigate. The marines discovered a hiding area behind a false bulkhead of the ship, dubbed the *Eagle,* which hid two naval deserters. Throughout the war, the Continental Navy had a problem with men deserting to serve on privateers, where the prize money was higher and the discipline lower. Most deserters got away. These two men were unfortunate enough to be captured. Jones not only seized the two deserters but also "drafted" twenty more men from the *Eagle*'s crew. This was not the last Jones would hear of the *Eagle.*

Jones made two major catches in this cruise. On the way to Nova Scotia, Jones and his crew boarded and captured the *Mellish.* This merchant ship carried silk, medicine, important British civilians, and 10,000 winter uniforms intended for the British army headed down the Hudson River in an attempt to split the American colonies. Jones wrote the Congressional Marine Committee in November: "The loss of the *Mellish* will distress the enemy more than can be easily imagined, as the clothing on board her is the last intended to be sent out for Canada this season."

On the voyage back, Jones captured a merchant ship loaded with coal for the British in New York. There is no indication of what Jones did with this ship, but the coal it carried would not go to the British army.

Jones was right on the mark about the importance of his capture. The British army, under command of General John Burgoyne, was hurt by not having winter uniforms.

The series of battles in the fall of 1777, which became known collectively as the battle of Saratoga, were a disaster for the British. Burgoyne eventually had to surrender his army. This defeat was one of the decisive turning points in the war, not least because it encouraged France, Great Britain's longtime enemy, to openly support the Americans.

Five

To France

Jones had a very unexpected surprise when he got back to Boston just before Christmas of 1776. He was nearly arrested. The owner of the *Eagle* had accused him of piracy in a complaint filed with Boston authorities. Soon after arriving in Boston, a lawyer and the sheriff approached Jones on the street. When the lawyer demanded that the sheriff arrest Jones, the captain drew his sword and threatened to use it on anyone who touched him. The lawyer then seemed to forget that independence had been declared and cried out that the sheriff was a "King's officer." The angry Jones responded, "Is he? By God, I have a commission then to take his head off." The sheriff, clearly starting to regret his decision to get involved, responded to Jones, "I ain't no king's officer."

The lawyer's response to that was an exasperated, "Why don't you take him?" The sheriff's retort was a very logical, "The Devil! Don't you see his poker [sword]!"

Jones's next step, after this brief comedy, was to write his lawyer to describe the incident. The lawyer, on Jones's behalf, then countersued the owners of the *Eagle,* and the case was eventually thrown out of court.

Jones was disappointed to learn that although he had captained two successful cruises, the navy had relieved him of the *Alfred*'s command and offered only a return to command of the smaller *Providence*. Congress had decided to draw up a list of captains but failed to establish a merit-based system of promotion. They based the order of the names of the captain's list, which represented their rank in the navy, solely on how much political influence each captain had. Jones was eighteenth on the list because his main supporter in Congress, Joseph Hewes, had been away when the list was created.

Jones did not blame Hewes for being away but, as could be expected, he did not take the news well. On January 12, 1777, he wrote Hewes: "That such despicable characters should have obtained commissions as commanders in a navy is truly astonishing and [might] pass for romance with me unless I have been convinced by my senses of the sad reality."

Regardless of the captains' list, Jones was attracting the attention of some influential members of Congress. In January 1777, Robert Morris wrote John Hancock, president of the Congress, to say Jones "is a fine fellow and should be constantly kept employed." Morris appreciated Jones's ideas of how the navy should be organized and operated, although he did not like Jones's constant complaining about mistreatment. Morris told Jones that his letters on naval operations were "always entertaining and in many parts useful." Morris could see that Jones brought a broader perspective to naval affairs than most other naval officers and members of Congress. While Jones was primarily interested in his own career, he was also interested in the navy, and knew that the only way he would rise in rank would be through his ideas, initiative, and courage.

On February 5, 1777, Morris wrote to Jones:

> It has long been clear to me that our infant fleet cannot protect our own coasts & that the only effectual relief it can afford us is to attack the enemies' defenseless places and thereby oblige them to station more of their ships in their own countries or to keep them employed in following ours . . . either way we are relieved.

Jones had already been thinking along the same lines. Inspired by this letter, he began to look for innovative ways to most effectively use the limited American naval resources against the British. He decided that diversionary hit-and-run raids on the enemy's coast were the best strategy. Public outcry at the raids on London and other cities would force the British to divert resources from

North America to defend their own homeland.

Jones wanted to ratchet up the stakes the British would have to pay to continue the war. This was a new strategy in warfare. War in the eighteenth century usually focused on the enemy's military. There had been massively destructive, anti-civilian wars of attrition in the past, such as the European religious wars of the fifteenth and sixteenth centuries, when thousands of innocent civilians died from violence, hunger, and disease. Neither Jones nor Morris wanted this sort of conflict. The colonies did not have the resources to carry a war onto the British homeland. But they did want to create a panic, even a terror, among enough British civilians and destroy enough of their property that they would pressure the Parliament and the king's ministers to end the war.

The first six months of 1777, spent waiting for an assignment to a ship, frustrated Jones. He was unable to get his name raised higher on the captains' list. In February, he was promised a small fleet to go after British bases in the Caribbean and the southern colonies, but Esek Hopkins, still the senior officer in the Navy, did not get the ships repaired. Jones protested so much and so virulently over the delay that Hopkins finally complained to the Continental Congress. But this action probably hurt Hopkins because the Congress had also been pressuring Hopkins to get the ships back into the fight. Hopkins was soon suspended from his position and then dismissed from the service.

Things seemed to be getting better for Jones in May 1777. Congress ordered him to proceed to New Hampshire and from there sail on a French ship for France, which was secretly aiding the Americans. Once in France, Jones was to take command of a "fine frigate," as it was described in his orders, being built for him there. However, the French captain refused to take Jones under the unusual conditions Congress required. Congress had insisted that Jones and the French captain share command in battle and share any prize money from the sale of captured enemy vessels.

It was July 2 before Jones set out for France. He received formal orders to go to Portsmouth, New Hampshire, to take command of the sloop *Ranger*. Jones would then proceed to France to pick up his new frigate. The *Ranger* would serve as escort for Jones in British waters.

Construction on a new ship was often delayed, and sometimes the captain would have to supervise its completion. This proved to be the case with the *Ranger,* which lacked sails and war material, including cannons. The ship also lacked a crew.

The *Ranger* was a twenty-gun sloop, small but fast. Equipping it and finding a crew proved to be a slow process. Most experienced seamen in the area had already signed on with privateers. When Jones arrived in New Hampshire, he already had recruiting posters printed and eventually collected a crew, mostly from New Hampshire and Massachusetts.

Jones was less successful with his officers. They were

GREAT
ENCOURAGEMENT
FOR
SEAMEN.

ALL GENTLEMEN SEAMEN and able-bodied LANDSMEN who have a Mind to distinguish themselves in the GLORIOUS CAUSE of their COUNTRY, and make their Fortunes, an Opportunity now offers on board the Ship RANGER, of Twenty Guns, (for FRANCE) now laying in PORTSMOUTH, in the State of NEW-HAMPSHIRE, commanded by JOHN PAUL JONES Esq; let them repair to the Ship's Rendezvous in PORTSMOUTH, or at the Sign of Commodore MANLEY, in SALEM, where they will be kindly entertained, and receive the greatest Encouragement.---The Ship RANGER, in the Opinion of every Person who has seen her is looked upon to be one of the best Cruizers in AMERICA.---She will be always able to Fight her Guns under a most excellent Cover; and no Vessel yet built was ever calculated for sailing faster, and making good Weather.

Any GENTLEMEN VOLUNTEERS who have a Mind to take an agreable Voyage in this pleasant Season of the Year, may, by entering on board the above Ship RANGER, meet with every Civility they can possibly expect, and for a further Encouragement depend on the first Opportunity being embraced to reward each one agreable to his Merit.

All reasonable Travelling Expences will be allowed, and the Advance-Money be paid on their Appearance on Board.

IN CONGRESS, MARCH 29, 1777.

RESOLVED,

THAT the MARINE COMMITTEE be authorised to advance to every able Seaman, that enters into the CONTINENTAL SERVICE, any Sum not exceeding FORTY DOLLARS, and to every ordinary Seaman or Landsman, any Sum not exceeding TWENTY DOLLARS, to be deducted from their future Prize-Money.

By Order of CONGRESS,
JOHN-HANCOCK, PRESIDENT.

DANVERS: Printed by E. RUSSELL, at the House late the Bell-Tavern.

A poster recruiting sailors to work on board the Ranger *under Jones's command.* (Library of Congress)

chosen for him by John Langdon, the *Ranger*'s politically connected builder, and William Whipple, the local congressman. First Lieutenant Thomas Simpson, the executive officer (second-ranking man on the ship, next to the captain) was Langdon's brother-in-law. Langdon could not find any proper canvas sails and they had to make do with the cheaper material used for gunnysacks. The masts and spars were too big, as it had been impossible to find logs of the proper size. Jones had the masts cut back, but the *Ranger* was still top heavy. In a stiff wind, it might tip over.

When he was not in action at sea, Jones's favorite activity on land, aside from complaining about how he was being treated, was romance. There are indications that by this period of his life Jones had been involved in a series of liaisons with various women. Jones would never marry, but he apparently never deprived himself of female companionship.

On November 1, 1777, the *Ranger* finally set out to sea. Jones managed to get past the British frigates patrolling the coast and headed into the Atlantic. The ship had a very important cargo—dispatches announcing the American victory at Saratoga. He and the members of Congress hoped that news of the American victory would push France towards openly supporting the American cause.

About halfway across the Atlantic, Jones's concerns about whether the *Ranger* was "crank," whether it might roll over in strong wind or a heavy sea and possibly sink, proved to be well founded. The ship almost rolled onto its side during a gale. Fortunately, the ship righted itself after a few scary moments.

As the *Ranger* neared the British coast, lookouts

An anonymous portrait of John Paul Jones as captain of the Ranger. (National Archives)

spied seventeen ships in the distance: a merchant convoy. The Americans gave chase and discovered a seventy-four gun British warship escorted the convoy. Had the *Ranger* been spotted, it would have been sunk; direct confrontation with the big ship was out of the question. Although it had not yet been sighted, the *Ranger* was too close to slip away. Jones tried something else—he had has ship fall in line with the merchant convoy.

An unidentified officer onboard the *Ranger* later wrote home: "Our captain took a very wise step, which was to heave to with the convoy." Jones heaved to the convoy until nightfall, and the British warship crew never noticed the extra ship. As the officer noted, "Had he suspected us to be Americans, we must have been captured." After slipping away under cover of darkness, the remainder of the trip passed uneventfully. The *Ranger* arrived at the French port of Nantes on December 2, 1777.

Jones arrived in a good mood, impressed with his crew. But he had another career disappointment waiting for him in France. The promised "fine frigate," under construction in a Dutch shipyard, would not be given to him. The Dutch, who owned it, had been pressured by the British not to sell the ship to the Americans.

Jones decided to try to make the best of a bad situation and wrote to the American commissioners in Paris, including Benjamin Franklin, to thank them for their efforts on his behalf. Surprisingly, Jones apparently recognized, or pretended to recognize, that losing the command of the ship was not a personal insult. Franklin and his associates, Arthur Lee and Silas Deane, who was later replaced by John Adams, were trying to obtain French assistance and support for the American cause.

Benjamin Franklin (center, facing front) *stands with dignitaries sent to welcome him upon his arrival in France as an envoy to the court of Louis XVI.* (Library of Congress)

Shortly after Christmas 1777, Jones left Nantes for Paris. He wanted to discuss future plans with the commissioners, who were effectively his bosses while he was in France. Jones hoped to get an entire squadron of ships to raid the British coastline. Psychological warfare was not his only goal. He also wanted to free Americans, particularly sailors, being held prisoner in British jails. He would free those he could reach directly, and take British hostages to trade for others.

Jones had earlier complained bitterly that privateers

and other American naval captains, were releasing British prisoners taken in naval actions. Jones wrote Robert Morris, "Were this base conduct practiced by those licensed robbers alone, 'I should have found within my soul one drop of patience,' but to find individuals in our navy affected with the same foul contagion racks me with distressing passions and covers me with shame!"

In Paris, Jones saw a city that was in many ways rich and opulent. It was said that every morning 7,000 barbers headed to the homes of rich, male clients, to wash, curl, and style their hair. He would also have seen a Paris covered by a layer of slime, a combination of unpleasant substances. Drinking the city water would have made him ill. He probably followed the practice of rich Parisians, who drank only bottled mineral water.

Jones did not stay in Paris long before heading to the wealthy suburb of Passy, now part of the city of Paris. His destination was the Hôtel Valentinois, two large mansions in Passy and the headquarters of the American delegation. Jacques-Donatien Leray de Chaumont had lent Valentinois to the Americans. Chaumont was a self-made multimillionaire who had used his wealth to buy influence and an aristocratic title, Duc de Chaumont. Chaumont fed off a deep grudge against the British Empire and a desire to corner the market on supplying the Americans with military supplies.

France funneled early aid to the Americans through private merchants such as Chaumont. The French government was eager to subvert British power but wished to work

Eighteenth-century Paris was known as Europe's cultural center and was an excellent place to make influential contacts. This view of the city was taken from the Pont Neuf, one of the many Parisian bridges that spans the Seine. (Library of Congress)

discretely until they could be sure they were not backing a losing cause. French leaders, in the court of an absolute monarch, had little sympathy for the republican ideals of the Americans. But their hatred and distrust of the British was more powerful than their enmity toward democracy. The final argument for those favoring active intervention was, as Congress had hoped, the American victory at Saratoga. Another ship with the good news actually beat Jones to France. But he did write a friend, "It is with great pleasure that I see the political system of almost every power in Europe changing in our favor since the news of our late successes."

An open treaty of alliance between France and the

United States was to be signed in February 1778. Benjamin Franklin is given the bulk of the credit for successfully negotiating the treaty.

Jones made the acquaintance of Edward Bancroft, Franklin's diplomatic secretary. Bancroft, who had access to all confidential dealings of the American delegation, was out to make a profit from the war. He was also a British spy, regularly sending copies of all correspondence and information on almost all plans, including Jones's, to the British government. Though he sometimes failed to communicate information about plans

Benjamin Franklin was an important ally of Jones as well as one of the most admired Americans of his time. (Yale University Art Gallery)

that would make him a profit, Bancroft kept the British well-informed. For example, none of the letters Franklin wrote to Congress during his first year in France made it to Philadelphia. All were intercepted, thanks to Bancroft's information. Fortunately for the American cause, this seems to have had little impact on the course of the war. Franklin seemed unconcerned about possibly being spied on and never suspected Bancroft. One incident, which should have given things away, passed unnoticed. The British ambassador to France protested a letter to the French foreign minister from the Americans before the foreign minister received the letter.

Jones became friendly with Bancroft and was very open about his plans. Bancroft tipped off the British about a raid Jones had planned in March 1778. Fortunately for Jones, the raid was cancelled. However, Bancroft did not tip off the British about Jones's August 1778 cruise. Bancroft had been known to withhold information about cruises when he had a commercial interest in the cargo. He might also have gone soft on his friend Jones. Jones apparently did not suspect him, although he did wonder in February why it was so hard to keep American plans secret.

By February, Jones was actively supervising repairs and upgrades to the *Ranger,* all the time hoping for command of a larger ship. His executive officer, First Lieutenant Simpson, was also hoping Jones would get a new command. Simpson had expected to take over the *Ranger* and sail it back to America.

In February, Jones and his ship received a formal military salute from a French warship, signifying French recognition of the United States as an independent nation. This was the first time a United States Navy ship had received a military salute from a foreign government.

On April 4, 1778, Jones wrote the three American commissioners that he was preparing to sail on a raid. He did not tell them where he was going, but they probably guessed he planned to operate in British waters. Jones had earlier written the Marine Committee of Congress, "When an enemy thinks a design against them improbable they can always be surprised and attacked with advantage."

Six

The Cruise of the *Ranger*

The *Ranger* left the French port of Brest on April 8, 1778, and entered the channel between England and Ireland on April 15. Jones thought there were less defensible targets in Ireland and along the west coast of England and Scotland. The spring weather was windy and overcast, which would have shielded potential targets from the Americans, but also would have shielded them from most British warships. Jones, trying to improve the *Ranger*'s performance, ordered his men to move around some ballast in the hull. Ballast was material, usually lead, kept in the hull of a ship to lower the center of gravity and make it less likely to tip over in a storm or heavy seas.

Jones planned to sail to the south coast of Scotland to the port of Whitehaven, to burn some of the merchant

ships docked there. He also planned to kidnap the Earl of Selkirk, whom he considered an important British nobleman living in the area, and hold him hostage to obtain the release of captive American seamen.

Jones knew the local waters; this was the area where he had gained his first sea experience. He served as his own pilot to guide the *Ranger* close to shore. He was also acquainted with the Selkirks. The earl's father had been the closest friend of William Craik, and a frequent visitor at the estate where Jones grew up. Jones might even have met the earl himself.

One also has to wonder whether Jones had personal motives, as well as strategic and operational reasons behind his plans. He had grown up in the area as a child of the working class. Perhaps, without realizing it himself, Jones was seeking revenge for his treatment at the hands of the aristocracy, in addition to helping his cause.

Jones's motives became irrelevant when he tried to put his plans into action. Continental leaders of the time tried to lead, but the men would not always follow. This was particularly true in the navy. American sailors were less likely to follow orders than sailors from more established countries. Occasionally, they even endangered military operations. New England sailors, such as those with Jones, came from perhaps the most democratic area of the country. They saw no reason why their town-meeting tradition, where every man had a say in what

Opposite: *The* Ranger *sailed out of the port of Brest, located in northwest France.* (National Maritime Museum, Greenwich, England)

happened in a town, had to be ignored just because they were at war. This was in stark contrast to the harsh discipline of the British Royal Navy, where officers doled out beatings or worse, for relatively minor offenses. American captains, on the other hand, although they theoretically could punish, usually had to alternate between persuading and bribing their crews.

The crew of the *Ranger* was not happy about raiding Britain. They thought they should be on their way back to America to sell the captured British merchant ships and to collect their prize money. Jones sensed pending problems and later wrote about "a slow and half obedience I had observed even from the beginning."

A few days after leaving France, Jones faced a mutiny. Jean Meijer, the French officer who had volunteered to command the marine detachment onboard ship, was the only officer that remained loyal to Jones. Meijer tipped him off about a pending mutiny. The ship's master, roughly equivalent to a senior noncommissioned officer in the modern navy, was supposed to take Jones captive. All other officers would make sure they were not around when this happened. The ship would then sail for America, with Jones either in chains or thrown overboard.

Jones had no proof that Meijer was telling him the truth. He decided to wait for something to happen. Then the master, David Cullam, rushed Jones, as Meijer had warned, while Jones paced the quarterdeck—the raised open area at the back of the ship. Jones pulled out his pistol and pointed it at Cullam's head, and the master and

This British caricature of John Paul Jones portrays him as a pirate, a reference to the terrifying raids along Britain's coasts for which he became notorious. (The Mariner's Museum, Newport News, Virginia)

his associates backed off. They were probably aware of his reputation for using deadly forces, as with the Ringleader early in his career.

Jones did not place Cullam in chains, which would have been appropriate, but the captain knew he now had to live with the ever-present possibility of a mutiny.

Before Jones, the last time Britain had been raided by a foreign power was in the seventeenth century, when a Dutch raiding party had burned a town on the southeast coast. The British people felt secure that this could not happen again because the "wooden walls" of the Royal Navy would protect them. Jones was determined to prove them wrong. It was a dangerous goal, but not impossible. Before the days of radar, when ships too far away to see were effectively invisible, a gap always existed in any defensive naval screen. The trick was finding it.

On April 17, the *Ranger* reached Whitehaven. Jones managed to assemble a thirty-man raiding party from a crew of 150. But when the crew lowered the boats into the water at about 10:00 PM, the wind both shifted and increased. Heavy waves broke on shore. The landing would now be far more risky. The *Ranger* risked either being wrecked on the rocks or becoming a sitting duck for any British warship that happened to pass by. Jones cancelled the raid and headed back to the open sea to await a better chance for success.

The next day Jones ran into the *Hussar,* a British revenue cutter (a small government ship employed to enforce revenue laws), on patrol for smugglers. In the battle that followed, the smaller *Hussar* was able to escape the *Ranger* by sailing into shallow waters close to shore, where the *Ranger* could not follow. Jones realized that once the British ship made port, an alarm would go out and any British warship in the area would pursue the Americans. Jones had to find targets of opportunity quickly.

Sailing west, Jones and his men captured a British fishing boat and interrogated its crew. They learned that the British sloop *Drake*, about the same size and firepower as the *Ranger,* lay in a harbor not far from Belfast, in what is now Northern Ireland. The *Drake*'s officers and crew were unlikely to have heard that the *Ranger* was in the area. Jones's first plan was to sail brazenly, during daylight, and sink or capture the British ship. However, according to a diary kept by the *Ranger*'s doctor, Ezra Green, the "people were unwilling to undertake it." No reason is given for the crew's refusal to obey these orders.

Jones negotiated an alternative plan with executive officer Simpson. The *Ranger* would enter the harbor at night and surprise the British ship. As the *Ranger* crossed the *Drake*'s bow, the American crew would throw grappling hooks over its side and use small arms to seize control.

The plan depended on the *Ranger* dropping anchor at just the right time next to the *Drake*, but the mate in charge of the anchor detail hesitated. The *Ranger* ended up one hundred feet in front of the *Drake,* too far for the plan to work. Jones ordered the *Ranger's* anchor cable cut—ships had several anchors, in anticipation of this method of getting underway quickly—and the *Ranger* first drifted and then sailed out of the harbor. Amazingly, the officers and crew of the *Drake* had no idea of the danger they had avoided.

Jones wanted to try again, but the tide had shifted and the ship could not get back into the harbor. He decided to raid Whitehaven again. As the *Ranger* sailed back toward the harbor, he told the crew his plans. He would lead a raiding party to capture the forts, spike the cannon, and then burn the merchantmen in the harbor. Not surprisingly, the officers and crew did not like this plan. Thomas Simpson, Jones's unreliable second in command, was one of the loudest objectors. The crew had signed on to earn prize money, not risk their lives trying to hurt the enemy where he lived. They told the captain they were too tired to perform their duties. Surgeon Green raised a more principled objection—the mission was dangerous and they would be attacking poor people's property. Jones was more responsive to Green's argument, but was still determined to go ahead with the raid.

The *Ranger* was behind schedule. By midnight of April 23, when he thought the attack would be under way, Jones was still several miles off shore. Boarding small boats, Jones and the thirty volunteers who joined him rowed ashore. But the sun was starting to come up. Jones wanted to proceed and headed to the forts with some of the men. Jones told the remainder to prepare

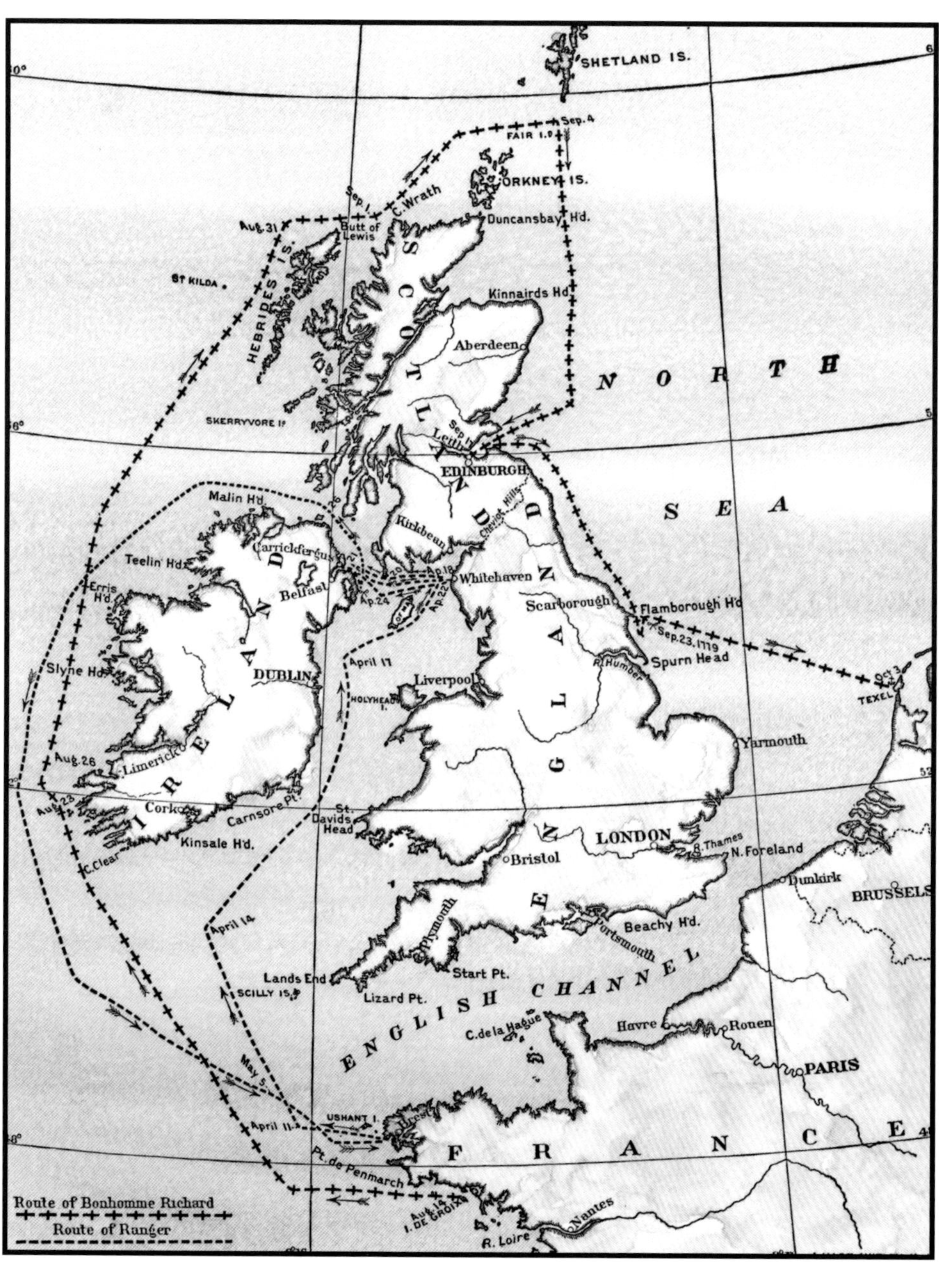

The cruise routes of the Ranger *and, later, the* Bonhomme Richard, *around the British Isles during the Revolutionary War.* (Courtesy of the North Wind Picture Archive.)

to burn the nearly two hundred vessels docked close together.

The raid on the fort went well. Jones and his raiding party quickly and efficiently slipped inside the walls, overcame the guards, and spiked the guns. Spiking consisting of driving heavy nails into cannon touch-holes used to fire the guns, which rendered them inoperable.

The sun was now coming over the horizon, but Jones still had some surprises left. He called for the rest of the men from the ship to join him. Many of those who came ashore had gotten drunk in the meantime. This turned out to be fortunate for Jones because they had been planning to leave him on shore but were now incapable of following through on their plan. After a bit of arguing about why the ships were not already on fire, Jones and the men headed out to find fire. They found a coal ship and threw a candle into it but nothing happened. Jones then had his men pour a barrel full of tar into the hold of the ship. Soon the ship was ablaze.

The town was now awake. One of Jones's seamen had enlisted in New Hampshire for the sole purpose of getting home to England and had no loyalty to the American cause. He banged on doors to warn the town of their danger. Citizens ran towards the docks to see what was happening. As Jones later described it:

> The inhabitants began to appear in thousands and individuals ran hastily towards us. I stood between

> them and the Ship of Fire with a pistol in my hand and ordered them to retire which they did with precipitation. The flames had already caught the rigging and began to ascend the main mast. The sun was a full hour's march above the [horizon], and as sleep no longer ruled the world . . . it was time to retire.

This time his men put more effort into rowing back to the *Ranger*.

Jones and his men had put on a dramatic show but had done very little damage. They had destroyed only one ship. He decided to go ahead with the second part of his plan—to kidnap the Earl of Selkirk. He sailed twenty miles across the Firth of Solway. The entrance channel was tricky, but Jones had sailed it before. By noon, his landing cutter had reached the beach. Twelve armed men accompanied him to shore, including Master Cullam.

After landing, Jones and his men were heading up the hill toward the Selkirk house when they ran into Lord Selkirk's gardener. Jones told the gardener that he and his men were a Royal Navy press gang. They had come ashore to draft men for the navy. It was an ingenious trick. The gardener immediately warned all young men on the estate to flee forced naval service. There was no one left to protect Selkirk. Unfortunately, Selkirk was not at home.

Disappointed, Jones turned to head back to the ship. Cullam and another officer stopped Jones, insisting they were not going back without something. They were sure there was treasure in the house, and demanded that

Jones let them go collect it. Jones faced a dilemma. If he agreed to their demand, he had no way of controlling the damage they might do. If he resisted, they would probably kill him and do the damage anyway. He compromised. The men would wait outside while the two officers went to get the Selkirk silver—the expensive dining-room plates, silverware, cups, and saucers. Jones decided to stay outside with Cullam and the others.

Most of the women and children in the house fled to the top floor. Lady Selkirk met the two officers, and acceded to their demands. She was not impressed with them, but later wrote her husband, "Upon the whole, I must say they behaved civilly."

Jones would have been more concerned for his reputation if he had read another paragraph in Lady Selkirk's letter. She had been told by one of the officers in her home that the captain of their ship was Jones. The letter goes on to say,

> It was immediately known that this Paul Jones is one John Paul, born at Arbigland, who once commanded a Kirkcudbright vessel belonging to Mr. Muir and others, a great villain as ever was born, guilty of many crimes and several murders by ill usage, was tried and condemned for one, escaped, and followed a piratical life, til he engaged with the Americans.

Jones and the *Ranger* deserted the area and headed back to northern Ireland. Jones was unhappy about the results of this phase of his cruise. He wanted one more try at capturing or sinking the *Drake*. Lieutenant Simpson made another effort to stir up the crew against Jones when the *Ranger* arrived at northern Ireland. Then, before the *Ranger*'s crew realized it, they had drifted into Carrickfergus Harbor. Ezra Green wrote, "The tide and what little wind there was had imperceptibly carried us in so far that there was very little chance for an escape."

This time the crew of the *Drake* was more alert. The British ship unfurled its sails in case it had to challenge the intruder. But first a boat came out to investigate. Jones was flying a British flag and trying to appear as a merchantman. Jones ordered the *Ranger*'s helmsman to turn the stern toward the longboat to keep the British from seeing the *Ranger*'s cannon. When the *Drake*'s boat came alongside, Jones, wearing a uniform identical to that of a British naval officer, greeted the British officer. He then informed the officer that he and his men were prisoners of the United States and took them below deck.

This served as a warning to the *Drake*. The American and British ships made their way out of the harbor. Jones wanted to fight in the open sea, where he would have more room to maneuver. Both ships were about evenly matched as to size and armaments. But the *Drake* had more men, an advantage if the ships got close enough for boarding. The *Drake* also had a more experienced crew. Jones knew the British crew was almost certainly

Fighting between the Ranger *and the* Drake *off the coast of Scotland. In this image, the* Ranger *is flying the American flag. Jones would have raised this flag once combat between the ships had begun.* (Library of Congress)

better disciplined than his own men.

The ships drew close, and the fighting began as the sun was going down. Sailors from both sides called out formal challenges, the custom in single-ship combat. Jones then sent marines up into the masts to shoot down any British crew on deck. When the *Ranger* crossed the *Drake*'s bow, Jones ordered his men to open fire with the nine guns on the side. Grapeshot, anti-personnel ammunition consisting of small iron balls, sliced down the *Drake*'s deck. When the small iron balls hit wood, they sent splinters flying, adding a dangerous, indirect shrapnel effect.

Now Jones's ship was vulnerable. It would take his men one or two minutes to reload. The *Drake*'s broadside could open up on the back, or the stern, of the *Ranger.* This could particularly endanger the officers, including Jones, standing by the helm near the stern of the ship. The custom of the day did not allow the officers to take cover. Jones knew this and ordered a quick turn. Both ships sat broadside to broadside.

Jones decided to make an effort to capture, rather than sink, the *Drake*. As the two ships sailed almost side by side, the *Ranger*'s broadside angled upwards so cannon shots could hopefully damage the *Drake*'s masts and spars. The *Drake*'s cannon angled downwards. Normally this might risk sinking the *Ranger*, but the *Drake's* cannon were smaller caliber, meaning they fired smaller and less powerful balls.

The ships bashed away at each other for an hour until the *Drake*'s masts and spars were nearly wrecked. Even worse, the captain and first lieutenant had been seriously wounded and could no longer exercise command. The sailing master realized he would have to surrender. For the first time in history, a United States Navy ship had won a single-ship combat against a Royal Navy ship.

Despite the relatively fierce combat, the British lost only four dead and nineteen wounded, the Americans three dead and five wounded. There is no indication of how many of the wounded died from the poor medical care of the day. Doctors, including Green, did their best, but the necessary technology and medical knowledge did not exist. For example, it would be almost a century before doctors realized they should wash their hands before surgery.

Jones had surprisingly little trouble getting back to France, at least from the British. After the crew had repaired the *Drake* enough to sail, Jones put Simpson and a prize crew on the ship to get it back to France. At the first opportunity, Simpson tried to sail away from the *Ranger.* Jones caught up with him and finally could take action because Simpson had disobeyed a direct written order to keep the *Drake* near the *Ranger.* Jones placed Simpson under arrest.

Jones was not too happy with the results of his cruise. After a series of mishaps resembling low comedy, he had burned only one coal ship, captured a warship and a few merchantman, and came away with some plates and silverware. But Jones had accomplished something far greater with the *Ranger.* He made the British public wonder about their own security.

Seven
The *Bonhomme Richard*

Jones and the *Ranger* received little notice when they arrived back at Brest on May 7, 1778. There had been no messages for him from the American commissioners for several weeks. His bank draft, drawn on the commissioners' funds, was even refused when he tried to use it to buy supplies for his men.

Jones finally heard from Benjamin Franklin at the end of May. Franklin warmly congratulated him on his success and arranged to get Jones some additional food and clothing for his men. Franklin soon raised another, less pleasant issue. He and the new commissioner, John Adams, who had replaced Silas Deane, asked Jones to release Thomas Simpson, still under arrest, and send him home with the *Ranger*. To Franklin's surprise, Jones agreed to let Simpson go. It was one way to get rid of

The palace at Versailles, just outside of Paris, was the seat of the French court. The palace was open to anyone who wished to visit; however, it was an extremely difficult and protracted process to gain an audience with the French royal family and other government officials. (Château de Versailles)

a disloyal officer and crew. The *Ranger* returned to America without him.

Jones had to wait a year before sailing on his next war patrol. He spent his time finding a ship, getting it ready for action, and recruiting a new crew. He also spent time socializing in Parisian society. He even tried to learn French, because very few of the French learned English.

Franklin instructed Jones to deal directly with the French Ministry of Marine, in charge of the French navy, to negotiate for the frigate Jones was still waiting to have delivered. Dealing with the French government required patience. Composer Wolfgang Amadeus Mozart, for example, arrived in March 1778 to see Queen Marie Antoinette. By September, he gave up and went home.

Jones was no more successful than Mozart. Nothing came of his meetings with the other French officials, who once again denied Jones the frigate. This actually might have saved his life, however, because George Bancroft, the British spy working for Franklin, reported that one of Jones's proposed cruises was going to happen. The British, acting on the tip and eager to revenge his attacks on their coastline, had several warships waiting for Jones, who fortunately did not show up.

By September 1778, the Duc de Chaumont began looking for a ship for Jones. He offered him a sloop, a ship similar to the *Ranger,* but Jones declined, writing Chaumont the famous words that he wished to "have no Connection with any Ship that does not sail *fast,* for I intend *to go in harm's way.*"

In December, Jones leaned of a ship for sale, the *Duc de Duras,* and went to take a look. The fourteen-year-old ship was not fast. It had sailed to China and back four times as an armed merchantman but could be refitted as a warship. The ship needed some work but had certain advantages. It was well-built and would be able to absorb cannon fire better than some others. Its beams and seams were worn but would not let in more water than the pumps could handle. In February 1779, the French government finally agreed to buy the ship for Jones. He immediately renamed it the *Bonhomme Richard*, after

Jones increased the firepower of the frigate Bonhomme Richard *to twenty guns per side during the ship's renovation.* (Library of Congress)

the French title of Franklin's famous work, *Poor Richard's Almanac*.

Jones spent the next six months outfitting his new ship, getting a crew, and deciding his next plan of attack. During this period, Jones confessed to Franklin and Bancroft about the incident with "the Ringleader." Jones thought they had heard the story from his enemies and wanted to clear the air. They had not heard it, and Franklin was surprised at the confession. There is no indication as to what the British government thought.

The French gave Jones command of a squadron of ships. The most significant of these was the American frigate *Alliance*. With thirty-six guns, it was almost as well armed as the *Bonhomme Richard*. Pierre Landais, a Frenchman with a commission as a Continental Navy captain, commanded the *Alliance*. John Adams, who met Landais before Jones did, wrote in his diary that the Frenchman was "jealous of everything. Jealous of everybody. . . . There is in this man an inactivity and an indecision that will ruin him. He is bewildered—an absent, bewildered man—an embarrassed mind."

Landais gave Jones a hint of his command ability during a shakedown cruise designed to test the rebuilt *Bonhomme Richard,* held near Brest the night of June 19, 1778. Landais, on deck, heard shouts and saw the *Bonhomme Richard* looming out of the darkness. Despite the fact that what he heard was probably the *Richard*'s crew warning him to get out of the way, Landais decided the crew had mutinied. While he went down to his cabin to get some pistols, the ships collided. Fortunately, the damage to both was repairable.

One interesting addition to the *Richard*'s crew was the presence of 140 French marines, who were actually Irish mercenaries serving with the French. Jones wanted strong and reliable landing forces in addition to plenty of sharpshooters in the masts during combat. Out of a total crew of 380, the *Richard* boasted a ratio of more than one marine to two sailors. Any budding mutinies would find it hard to gain traction. On August 14, 1779, Jones's squadron went to sea.

Jones's cruise acted as a diversion for a larger operation. Great Britain had declared war on France after learning of the alliance between France and the United

States. By 1779, Spain was also at war with the British. Both countries wanted to avenge past defeats by the British, which was the primary reason two absolute monarchies were supporting a democratic revolution.

The strategic plan called for a large combined French-Spanish fleet to first win control of the English Channel from the British, and then to land a large raiding force on the southwest coast of Britain. However, the raid was called off before any fighting occurred due to epidemic disease on the French and Spanish ships. Jones sailed on, heading west around Ireland, with the *Bonhomme Richard,* the slowest of his five major ships, bringing up the rear. Two privateers sailed with the small fleet part of the time, staying close when their captains felt it was best.

Some days out, due to lack of wind, the *Richard* became becalmed—with no wind to fill the sails, at the mercy of the current. Jones sent the captain's barge, an oar-powered boat, with a towline to pull his ship to safety. The crew of the barge decided not to follow orders but to cut the towline and head towards shore. They never returned, nor did the longboat. Jones, angry at the desertion, particularly in the small boat kept on the ship for the captain's use, sent a party after them.

The next day, Jones ordered the smaller cutter *Cerf,* which had a shallow draft, to sail in toward shore to see if it could spot potential prizes. Suddenly, a gale blew up and the *Cerf* vanished. This ship might have deserted or been lost in the storm. A member of the crew later reported that the *Richard*'s pumps could barely keep up during the storm.

Captain Landais came to visit Jones on the afternoon of August 25. As commander of the second biggest ship in the fleet behind the *Bonhomme Richard,* Landais might be considered second in command of the entire squadron and mission. Jones generally did not make an effort to get along with his senior officers, but it's doubtful anything would have worked with Captain Landais. He was in a bad mood during this visit because Jones had forbidden Landais from chasing a potential prize into rocky waters near the coast. As Jones later wrote, Landais "was determined to follow his own opinion in chasing when and where he thought proper and in every other matter."

Jones tried to reason with Landais. He took the Frenchman by the hand and escorted him to his cabin, where he told Landais that he considered him to be a friend. The conversation turned ugly. Jones complained about his lost boats, and Landais said it was Jones's fault for sending them out in a fog. Jones muttered the words "That's a damn lie." By custom of the time, that statement meant Jones had called him a liar. In doing so, Jones had questioned Landais's honor, a serious offense that served as an invitation to a duel. That is exactly how Landais took it; Jones said they could not fight then but that he would be happy to fight when they got back on dry land. They parted enemies. Landais, from that point on, ignored Jones's orders, vanishing and returning when he felt like it. When it came time to fight, Landais would cause more trouble.

A second problem arose from the imprecise way in which Jones's order were drafted. Chaumont had told Jones the squadron was only to take prizes, not to stage landings. The French government thought this would be a better distraction from the planned invasion because the British would not know exactly where Jones was. Raiding a town would pinpoint his location. This order pleased the other captains, who wanted to concentrate on seizing prizes.

Jones wanted to stage raids. He had manned his ship with more than double the customary compliment of marines so they could function as ground troops. Besides, the *Bonhomme Richard* was slow and unlikely to catch too many British ships.

The British coast was far more alert than it had been, due both to Jones's earlier adventures and the reports of an approaching invasion fleet. The British did not know that disease had ravaged the French-Spanish fleet, leaving it essentially harmless. The land war in America had stalemated. Neither side could defeat the other, though the fighting was beginning to move south, where it would become more violent and involve more civilians. British civilians feared the Americans might retaliate and bring a vicious ground war to their own territory.

That was precisely what Jones was planning. He decided to raid Leith, the port city near Edinburgh, Scotland's capital. On September 14, 1779, his fleet arrived at the mouth of the Firth of Forth, the narrow bay leading to Edinburgh. The British defended Leith lightly, and Jones planned to hold the town for financial ransom with the goal of forcing the release of American seamen held in Britain. The financial ransom would be used to gain the promise of cooperation from the other two ships still with the squadron. The city leaders of Leith would be given a half hour to accept the ransom or Jones would burn Leith.

On September 16, the squadron began to slip up the firth. At one point, a cutter mistook the *Richard* for a British warship and asked Jones if he could spare a barrel of gunpowder. Jones gave them the gunpowder and asked to borrow the cutter's pilot in exchange. When the pilot came aboard, he was rather shocked to find himself in the presence of the "pirate" John Paul Jones.

Jones's efforts to hide his identity, by flying British flags and having the officers wear British uniforms, fooled few people. A letter by an unknown author, sent to the senior British officer in Edinburgh, describes meeting two of Jones's ships: "It is the opinion that they are both ships belonging to the enemy." A British officer, sent to take a look reported, "They are certainly the squadron of Paul Jones."

Families fled the approach of the notorious "pirate." Young men tried to find the few weapons still available to fight off the invaders. An aging Presbyterian minister went to the shore, put a chair in the surf, sat down, and prayed for a strong wind to blow the Americans away.

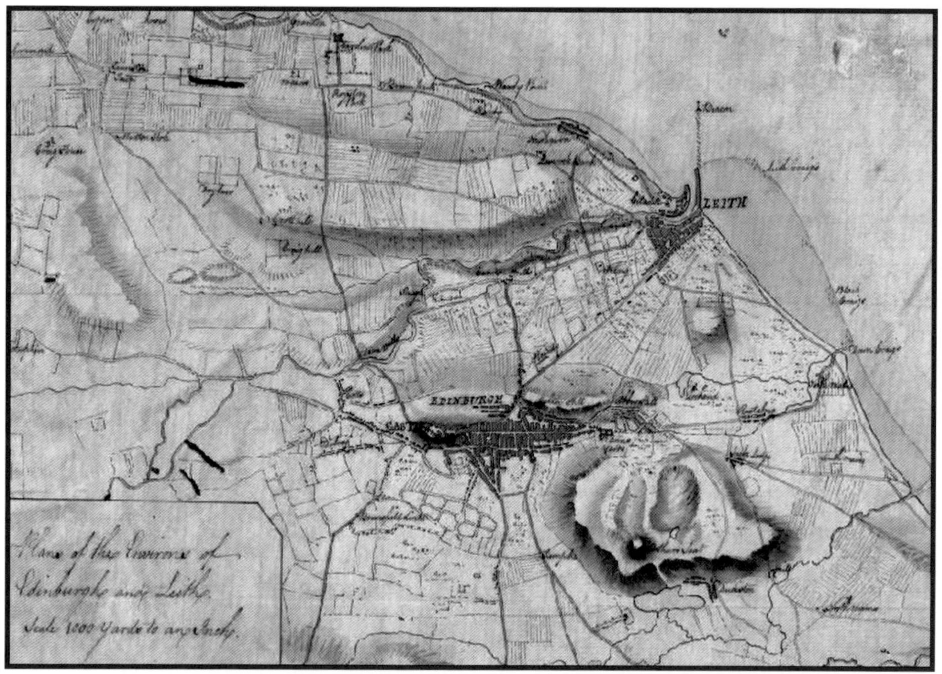

The port city of Leith, located on the Firth of Forth in eastern Scotland, was in a strategic position to protect the city of Edinburgh from a naval attack. (Library of Congress)

Jones had planned a dawn raid on Leith for September 17, but when he began embarking marines at 4:00 AM, the wind picked up, blowing away from Leith. The winds quickly increased to a full-fledged gale, and heavy rains came down from the Scottish highlands. The ships could make no further progress, nor could marines land.

There was nothing to do but head back to sea. Jones fired a parting cannon shot at a castle down the coast. He then considered another raid on Newcastle, the center of the British coal industry. Burning Newcastle's coal ships and keeping the British from carrying coal from

Newcastle to London would hurt the British war effort. But the other captains warned that this was too dangerous because word had already spread that they were in the area and the British might be waiting. Jones realized they were correct.

Jones was running short of time. His orders called for him to be in Holland by the first of October to escort a fleet of merchantmen to France, an important duty during wartime. On September 23, 1779, Jones paced the deck of the *Bonhomme Richard* as his squadron headed south towards the sea, near an area called Flamborough Head. Twenty miles to the north, Richard Pearson, the British captain of the *Serapis*, also paced his ship's deck.

Eight

"I Have Not Yet Begun to Fight"

Richard Pearson was a highly qualified captain and a worthy opponent for John Paul Jones. He was a veteran of thirty years at sea. If he had begun serving at about the same age as Jones, this would place him in his early forties by 1779. Pearson had been a captain for six years, giving him more military experience than Jones, but less total experience commanding a vessel because Jones had been a merchant captain. Pearson rose to captain at least partly on merit, though position and contacts were always a factor in the British Navy. He was sailing a newer, faster, and better-armed ship that had experienced officers and almost certainly a more disciplined crew.

The *Serapis* and a much smaller second ship, the *Countess of Scarborough,* were escorting forty-four merchant ships from Scandinavia to dockyards in southern

Captain Sir Richard Pearson, commander of the Royal Navy ship the Serapis. (National Maritime Museum, Greenwich, England)

England. The merchantmen carried valuable naval stores, such as timber, rope, and canvas, to be used for ship construction. Pearson knew Jones was somewhere in the area, but everything looked calm on the morning of September 23.

At 10:00 AM Pearson saw a red flag flying from Scarborough Castle. The red flag was a signal for "Enemy on Our Shores." A few minutes later, a fishing boat brought a message—several enemy ships had been spotted heading south the day before. That was an old message. Jones's squadron had actually turned around and was on its way back north, searching for the merchantmen. The lookouts of the *Serapis* spotted the four ships at 1:00 PM. They also spotted a signal from several merchantmen closer to Jones announcing the presence of unknown ships. Pearson sent the merchant ships closer to shore, where the guns at Scarborough castle could better protect them. He then moved *Serapis* and *Countess of Scarborough* between the merchant ships and the approaching American fleet.

The *Bonhomme Richard* was getting an equally good look at its adversary. The merchantmen, protected by the gun ships, were trying to flee to safety, and Jones wanted to get to them first. An observer later wrote, "As soon as Jones had taken a peep or two at them with his spyglass, he expressed himself to his officers, then standing by him upon the quarterdeck. This is the very fleet I have been so long cruising for."

The British merchant fleet before him was sometimes

called the Baltic Fleet. Some months before, Jones had proposed a plan to go after this fleet. He now had his chance. Jones signaled his other ships to give chase after the merchant ships. He needn't have bothered. His captains were already on their way.

The opposing ships closed very slowly. Running against a current, the Americans moved only a knot or two per hour. A tricky part of naval warfare at the time was how long it took the ships to get within range. This gave a lot of time to plan, but also gave the men a lot of time to consider the impending combat.

By 4:00 PM, Jones could see that he was facing a Royal Navy warship at least as big as his own. Around five, the marine drummers began to tap out "Beat to Quarters," the equivalent of the modern cry of "battle stations." Jones briefed his senior officers, always a questionable effort, but this group of officers was far more reliable than those Jones had earlier on the *Ranger*.

Jones aimed his guns at the enemy's rigging and hull. During combat, the hull of a warship would rock back and forth from the motion of the sea, changing the angle of the guns. A ship shot with the guns angled upwards, a French practice, to disable the rigging and prepare for boarding. By contrast, the British angled their guns down to sink the ship.

Two hundred years before, when they fought the Spanish, the British had smaller crews but better gunmen. Their tactic was to stand off and try to sink the enemy. The Spanish would try to get in close and board

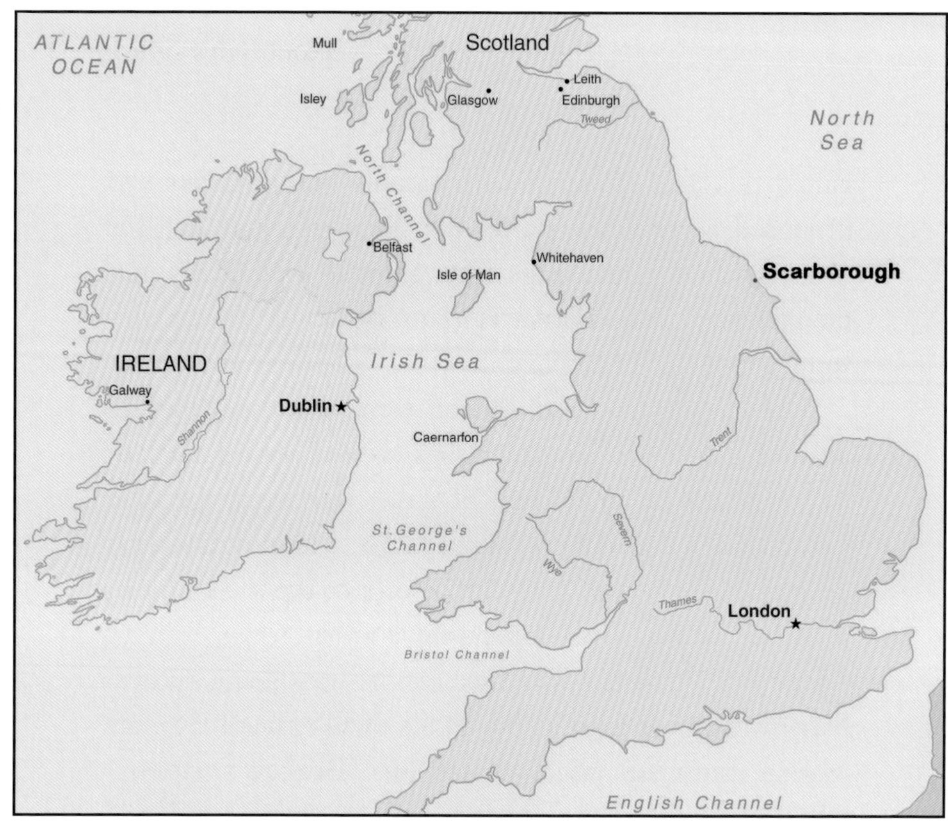

Jones fought the Serapis *near Scarborough, off England's east coast.*

their ships. Jones seemed to be combining the methods. Jones also planned for heavier-than-usual rifle fire from his marines. The *Richard* had been built to an older design than its opponent, with a high poop deck in the back. From there, marines could lay down a good field of fire on the quarterdeck—the command area—of the *Serapis*. Jones also put forty marines and seamen into what were called the "tops," or elevated firing platforms. They were instructed first to clear the British tops, to protect his men from being shot. Then they were to force all the crew off the *Serapis* deck.

The men in the tops were given a variety of weapons,

including small mortars (called coehorns) and baskets of grenades. Grenades were still popular in those days of single-shot pistols and rifles that took a long time to reload. They went out of common use in the nineteenth century but became popular again in the twentieth.

Interestingly, as one of the junior officers noted, "The captains of the tops drew into the tops a double allowance of grog for their men."

It began to get dark. About 6:00 PM, Jones could see the two British warships turning around and heading toward him, while still keeping between the Americans and the merchantmen. Jones signaled his other captains to form a line of battle. This was a common naval battle tactic of the time, enabling warships to fire broadsides at an enemy target one after the other. Unfortunately, if the enemy had more than one ship it could do the same in retaliation. A variation, which soon developed, was "crossing the t," cutting through the enemy's line of battle and firing broadsides at their more poorly defended bows and sterns. Jones's other captains, predictably, seemed to ignore his signal to form a line. It is possible, though, in the growing dark they did not see his signal.

Jones saw the *Serapis* open its gun ports. He knew that he was outgunned, slightly in numbers and more importantly in size. Jones also knew that his larger French-made guns might not be that reliable after heavy use; they might even blow up. Fired at close range, the British eighteen-pound gun, named for the weight of the ball it could fire, could go right through an enemy ship.

Jones saw Pearson on the deck of the *Serapis*. The back of the ship had lost its flagpole, along with the Royal Navy ensign, the naval version of the national flag. Pearson was nailing a new flag to the pole, larger than the old white flag with the British cross in the upper left. The new flag had a blood-red British cross covering the entire flag. Pearson was sending the message that the ship would not surrender by "striking," or lowering, its flag. The flag now could not be lowered.

Pearson had a good idea whom he was facing. However, Jones was still flying British colors. When the ships got close enough, Pearson asked what ship it was. Jones responded that it was the *Princess Royal,* a British merchantman about the same size as his ship. Pearson then asked where the ship came from. Jones pretended he could not hear. Pearson responded, "Tell me instantly from whence you came and who you be, or I'll fire a broadside into you!"

Jones had stalled all he could. The *Richard* raised the Continental naval flag. Then a nervous Continental marine fired his musket and both ships fired close-range broadsides. At the range of only twenty-five yards, every shot hit something, or someone. The sound must have been appalling, with all the cannon and small arms going off at the same time as well as the crack when something hit wood or the clanking when metal was struck. Adding to the danger, wood splinters were flying around the decks, becoming almost as much a hazard as the balls and bullets themselves.

The *Serapis* fired a second broadside, and one or two—no one ever knew for certain—of the *Richard*'s eighteen-pound guns blew up. The blast ripped a chunk out of the ship on the starboard side (the right side of the ship, looking forward; port is to the left). The explosion wrecked the gunroom, and Jones ordered it abandoned. Between this and the explosion, he lost almost half his heavy firepower. The ten eighteen-pound cannons on the port side of the *Serapis*, however, still worked and were still firing and doing damage.

Both ships maneuvered. Pearson managed to get in back of Jones and was able to rake the *Richard* in the stern with what was effectively a broadside, though the guns did not all fire at once. Pearson managed to get off two more effective broadsides, wrecking Jones's beautiful captain's cabin.

The *Serapis* was clearly winning the battle, with Pearson using his superior firepower and maneuverability to good advantage. Twenty-two of the twenty-five marines Jones had placed on the poop deck died or suffered wounds. Overturned guns lay scattered throughout the ship. Dr. Green had trouble keeping up with the stream of badly wounded men. One junior officer later wrote, "She made a dreadful havoc of our crew. Men were falling in all parts of the ship by the scores." Jones himself wrote in his official report, "I must confess that the enemy's ship being much more manageable than the *Bonhomme Richard* gained thereby several times an advantageous situation in spite of my best endeavors to prevent it."

Pearson punched holes in his opponent, literally. The *Serapis* fired a broadside approximately every two minutes. Some of the shots actually went all the way through the American ship. Jones knew he was losing, and knew he had to change the nature of the battle or his ship would sink. His chance came about an hour into the fight.

As Pearson tried to cross the *Richard*'s bow and rake it, the wind died. Jones sent his ship forward until it brushed against the *Serapis*. He then ordered grappling hooks to hold the two ships together to enable a party to board. The British resisted fiercely, though, and Jones saw that it would be a virtual suicide mission. The crew cut the ropes, and the *Richard* drew off.

A colorful depiction of the engagement between the Serapis *and the* Bonhomme Richard. (Library of Congress)

In the next few minutes of fighting, the *Serapis* fired a brutally destructive broadside. Jones then attempted to rake the *Serapis*'s bow, but his damaged ship couldn't pull off the maneuver. The *Serapis* lightly rammed the *Richard*.

Then fortune smiled on Jones. A small sail from the front of the *Serapis* fell onto the *Richard,* connecting it to the British ship. Jones immediately ordered the two ships tied together and then asked the sailing master to find a strong line to bind the ships more closely. Pearson realized the danger he was in and tried to drop anchor and break free. He could then deliver what he thought would be the final broadsides and sink the *Richard*.

Jones had his men throw grappling hooks to bind the ships together and ordered his marines to shoot the British sailors when they tried to cut the ropes or release the hooks. Then the spare anchor of the *Serapis* snagged on the *Richard;* the two ships were stuck together. It was going to be a fight to the death.

The two ships had battled for over an hour. Because it was relatively close to shore, a crowd had gathered to watch. A yellowish cloud of potentially deadly sulfuric smoke covered the two ships. Flashes of light would occasionally be visible as cannons were fired.

The battle became two fights. Pearson was still winning the one below decks, as his heavy guns continued to punch holes into the *Richard.* Frequently it cut two holes per shot, as balls went all the way through. The American heavy guns were silenced one by one. On deck, however,

American small arms fire was gradually killing or wounding everyone on the upper deck of the British warship. The heavy small-arms fire forced Captain Pearson to violate custom and take refuge below the quarterdeck command area.

Fire blazed on both ships. About 9:00 PM, almost two hours into the fight, the shooting died down as both crews concentrated on fighting the fires. Jones had time to notice that the *Pallas*, one of his companion ships, was actually doing some fighting against the *Countess of Scarborough*, and was on the verge of winning.

Jones soon found out what had happened to the *Alliance* and Captain Landais when the ship suddenly appeared and fired a broadside of anti-personnel grapeshot into both the *Serapis* and the *Bonhomme Richard*. The Americans were yelling "wrong ship" as the *Alliance* passed for another broadside and then vanished into the night. Jones had signal lanterns hung to try to let Landais know which ship he should not shoot at, if Landais decided to rejoin the action.

The *Bonhomme Richard* was slowly sinking. The ship's carpenter, John Gunnison, went into the hold to check and ended up to his chin in water. Back on deck, looking for an officer, all he could find was gunner's mate Henry Gardner. Gardner decided he was the ranking officer left alive and that the ship would have to give up. Gardner cried out the word for surrender, "Quarters."

Opposite: *Sailors engaged in hand-to-hand combat as the battle raged.* (Courtesy of the North Wind Picture Archive.)

Jones heard, and spun around yelling, "Who are those rascals? Shoot them! Kill them!" He then lunged at Gardner and Gunnison. The men saw that Jones was drawing his pistol, and they also saw the look in his eyes. The enraged Jones tried to shoot Gunnison, but his gun was empty. He then threw the pistol at Gardner, hitting him on the head and knocking him out.

Pearson had also heard the cries for "Quarters!" He went to the rail of his quarterdeck and asked, "Have you struck? Do you call for Quarters?" Jones's response earned him his place in American legend. He reported to Franklin that he answered Pearson "in the most determined negative." A contemporary report had Jones responding "I may sink, but I'll be damned if I strike." One of Jones's ranking subordinates, writing forty-five years later, reported the version of Jones's response that has gone down in history: "I have not yet begun to fight!"

Not long afterwards, the American master of arms took pity on British prisoners captured earlier that were confined in the hold where they faced drowning, so he released them. When a hundred or so British prisoners came up on deck, they were so grateful to be alive that Jones just needed a wave of his pistol to convince them to work the pumps.

A few minutes later, a party of about thirty armed British seamen and marines boarded. The *Richard*'s men fought them off to retreat. Then Landais came back about 10:00 PM to fire another broadside at both ships.

Captain Jones exchanges words with Pearson from his quarterdeck, relaying his most famous, and perhaps misremembered quote: "I have not yet begun to fight." (Courtesy of Art Resource.)

Twenty American sailors and marines had been effective firing from the top spar connected to the main mast of the *Richard.* They cleared the outside deck of the *Serapis* by shooting at anyone they could see. But their position was precarious, caught between damage to the main mast and fire. The position provided another opportunity. The mainsail yard, the crossbeam, extended over the deck of the *Serapis.* One sailor, a Scotsman named William Hamilton, collected a slow-burning match and basket of grenades. (The grenades had to be lighted and took twenty seconds for the fuse to burn.) Hamilton saw a half-open hatch on the *Serapis* and began dispatching live grenades into the hatch.

After the third grenade, Hamilton heard a loud bang

and then a series of thunderous explosions. Gun crews never wanted to leave gunpowder cartridges, which provided the propulsive power for cannon balls, lying around. But during this three-hour battle, the boys (literally boys—they were about twelve or thirteen) on the British ship must have got ahead of the gun crews. Many powder bags lying around exploded. A flash fire raced through the deck, badly burning many of the British sailors serving the guns. Pearson had lost five of his big guns. A sizable portion of his crew and his ship was on fire. He was close to losing his mainmast, which did collapse not long after the fighting stopped.

Suddenly, Pearson had no alternative but to surrender. When Jones did not fully hear Pearson's request, he asked him to strike his flag. Pearson, who had nailed up the flag, now had to rip it down nail by nail. Then there was the problem of getting word to the men to stop firing. A British sailor who did not know fighting had ceased brandished a pike and impaled the leader of a party of Americans sent to secure the *Serapis*.

Casualties were far higher than average naval battles of the day. Exact numbers are not known, but the figure probably ran close to 50 percent of both ships' crews. The *Bonhomme Richard* became one of the casualties. It was near blowing up as flames crept close to the gunpowder supplies. British officers volunteered to join in the human chain to move the powder to safer locations. If the ship exploded, it probably would have killed everyone on both ships. But there was no saving it. On the night of September 24, 1778, Jones ordered everyone off the *Bonhomme Richard* and onto the *Serapis*. The *Bonhomme Richard* sank a few moments later.

Nine

The Letdown

Jones had no way to know that the battle against the *Serapis* was his last action under the American flag. The remainder of his career, and the rest of his life, was an anticlimax.

For a while he was too busy to think about the future. He had won a heroic, if lucky, victory. But Jones now had to escape the British coast before more enemy ships arrived. British warships did arrive at Flamborough Head just after Jones and his squadron passed safely over the horizon, but they were unable to find Jones. Ten days later, he dropped anchor at Texel Island, just off Amsterdam.

There Jones discovered he had become famous. The *London Morning Post* reported that "Paul Jones resembles a Jack o' Lantern, to mislead our mariners and terrify our

Agreement between John Paul Jones and Captain Pearson.

It is hereby agreed between John Paul Jones, captain in the American navy, commander of the Continental squadron, now in the road of Texel, and Richard Pearson, captain in the British navy, late commodore of the British Baltic fleet, and now a prisoner of war to the United States of North America, as follows:

First. Captain Jones freely consents, *in behalf of the United States*, to land on the island of Texel the dangerously wounded prisoners now in his hands, to be there supported and provided with good surgeons and medicine at the expense of the United States of America, and, agreeable to the permission which he has received from the States-General of Holland, to guard them with sentinel in the fort on the Texel, with liberty to remove them from thence at his free will and pleasure.

Second. Captain Pearson engages, *in behalf of the British Government*, that all the British prisoners that may be landed as mentioned in the last article shall be considered afterwards as prisoners of war to the United States of America until they are exchanged, except only such as may in the mean time die of their wounds.

Third. Captain Pearson further engages, *in behalf of the British Government*, that, should any of the British subjects now prisoners of war in the hands of Captain Jones desert or abscond, either from the fort on the Texel or otherwise, in consequence of the first article, an equal number of American prisoners shall be released and sent from England to France by the next cartel.

Fourth. And Captain Jones engages, *on the part of the United States*, that if any of the prisoners who shall be landed should die while on shore in his custody in the fort, no exchange of them shall be claimed.

Done on board the American frigate the *Pallas*, at anchor in the Texel, this 3d day of October, 1779.

R. PEARSON.
JOHN PAUL JONES.

This 1779 agreement between Jones and Pearson was republished in 1888 as part of a compilation of diplomatic correspondence during the American Revolution. (Library of Congress)

coasts. He is no sooner seen than lost." Six of the prisoners freed from the *Bonhomme Richard* had managed to steal a boat and reach shore. They gave a reasonably accurate version of Jones throwing his pistol at the ship's carpenter, who had tried to strike the American flag. However, the tale appeared in the newspaper as:

During the engagement, Paul Jones (who was

> dressed in a short jacket and long trousers with about twelve charged pistols slung in a belt around his middle and a cutlass in his hand) shot seven of his men for deserting from their quarters, and to his nephew, whom he thought a little dastardly, he said that damn his eyes he would not blow his brains out, but he would pepper his shins, and actually had the barbarity to shoot at the lad's legs, who is a lieutenant in his ship.

The legend of John Paul Jones had begun.

Meanwhile, Jones wrote his report to Benjamin Franklin. Always a self-promoter, he distributed copies to Congress and placed selections in the press.

He had other, less pleasant matters to deal with as well. One was the conduct of Captain Landais during the fight with the *Serapis*. Jones was not inclined to give Landais the benefit of the doubt. Historians later thought it more likely that Landais was just confused when he fired at the *Serapis* with the *Bonhomme Richard* so close.

Three days after he arrived at Texel, Jones rowed into Amsterdam to arrange a prisoner exchange with British representatives. He had taken over five hundred British prisoners. The former crew of the *Bonhomme Richard* gave Jones three cheers as he left the ship. This crew was far more reliable than his previous crews. The exchange negotiations went nowhere. Three months later, to Jones's great annoyance, the French traded the prisoners for an equal number of French prisoners in British jails.

His men became angry at Jones for apparently relaxing

The port city of Amsterdam, where Jones relaxed and recuperated after winning the battle against the Serapis. (Courtesy of Art Resource.)

in Amsterdam while neglecting them, although part of the trip to Amsterdam was to try to arrange the prisoner exchange. But while in the city, he reveled in his new worldwide fame. He found his reputation particularly useful with women. Ever aware of his reputation, Jones took to heart a letter from a contact in Amsterdam who had written about some "great friends of America" and reported:

> Their feeling is that you have not done wrong, sir, to come and show yourself over here; but on the other hand they feel that it would not be right to repeat this visit, because it would amount to too much parading, and that would look bad even among the friends of America to see you visit especially public places.

By November, Jones faced political problems. He had brought his fleet into a neutral port, but the British were pressuring the Dutch to expel Jones so they could capture him with the fleet they had blockading Texel. The French wanted the Dutch to remain neutral and let Jones stay. They also wanted to be able to ship goods past the British blockade of their coasts on Dutch ships. Great Britain eventually declared war on the Netherlands on December 20, 1780, out of frustration.

Jones was told that the *Serapis* and two of his three other ships were going under French command. The French also took control of his prizes. He was now merely the captain of the *Alliance*. Jones did not take this well. Before transferring to the *Alliance,* he took all the movable supplies his men could carry from the prize ships.

By mid-December, the Dutch, still trying to avoid going to war with the British, grew tired of trying to persuade Jones to leave Texel. They sent a squadron, including a seventy-four gun ship to intimidate him. Jones did not respond. However, on Christmas Eve, a heavy gale blew the British fleet waiting for him off

John Paul Jones became captain of the Alliance *after losing his command over the* Serapis *and two of his three other ships.* (Courtesy of the North Wind Picture Archive.)

station. He seized the opportunity and brazenly zoomed his way past the British, sailing directly down the Dutch and French coasts.

Over the next few months, all of the old problems returned to haunt Jones. Due both to his personality and lack of emotional control, as well as some other circumstances, Jones's crew began to turn against him. Another problem was that by January 1780, they had still not been paid salary or prize money. He was able to get them some funds, and informed them he had also not been paid. (The crew of the *Bonhomme Richard* did not receive final prize money until 1848, voted to them by Congress, by which time they all were dead. Congress paid the money to their families.)

Jones's experience with the *Alliance* came to an almost comical ending. By the middle of June, after several months spent seeking pay for his men, complaining about how he was being treated, and romancing women, he was back on board *Alliance*, which was finally ready to sail for America with a load of arms and uniforms supplied by the French. By then, amazingly enough, Captain Landais had declared himself back in command of the ship. For reasons that remain unclear, Jones took no action and let the ship sail under Landais.

When he learned from George Bancroft that Jones had complained about lack of French support in his claim against Landais, Benjamin Franklin sent Jones a strongly worded letter:

> If you had stayed aboard where your duty lay you would not have lost your ship. . . . Hereafter, if you should observe on occasion to give your officers and friends a little more praise than is their due, and confess more fault than you can justly be charged with, you will only become the sooner for it, a great captain. Criticizing and censuring almost everyone you have to do with, will diminish friends, increase enemies, and thereby hurt your affairs.

After the usual period of waiting for a command, and a short but unsuccessful cruise on another ship, the *Ariel*, Jones finally made it back to America in February 1781. He then tried to have himself appointed as America's first admiral. He had come back from France a chevalier, equivalent to a British knight, in reward for services. He now wanted an equal reward from his own country. But political maneuvering by some rival captains who envied Jones's success prevented him from getting the rank.

Instead, he was promised command of the *America*, a seventy-four gun ship of the line the Americans were building. But the war ended before construction was completed. Congress gave the *America* to the French not long after the war because the government could not afford such a large ship and thought it was no longer needed.

Jones was unable to get his promotion or interest Congress in using money it probably did not have to pay for an expanded United States Navy. He was able to persuade Congress to send him to Paris in pursuit of prize money owed from the cruises of the *Ranger* and the *Bonhomme Richard*. He departed for France on November 10, 1784. He decided to leave at home one of his prize possessions: the inscribed sword that Louis XVI had given him when he was made a chevalier.

Major Pierre L'Enfant, who was headed back to France after service in America, joined Jones on the trip. L'Enfant was similar to Jones in one way. A highly skilled engineering officer, L'Enfant would eventually design Washington, DC, creating the basis for the city layout that still exists today. But his personality was so prickly that he was eventually fired and did not get to handle the actual surveying of the city.

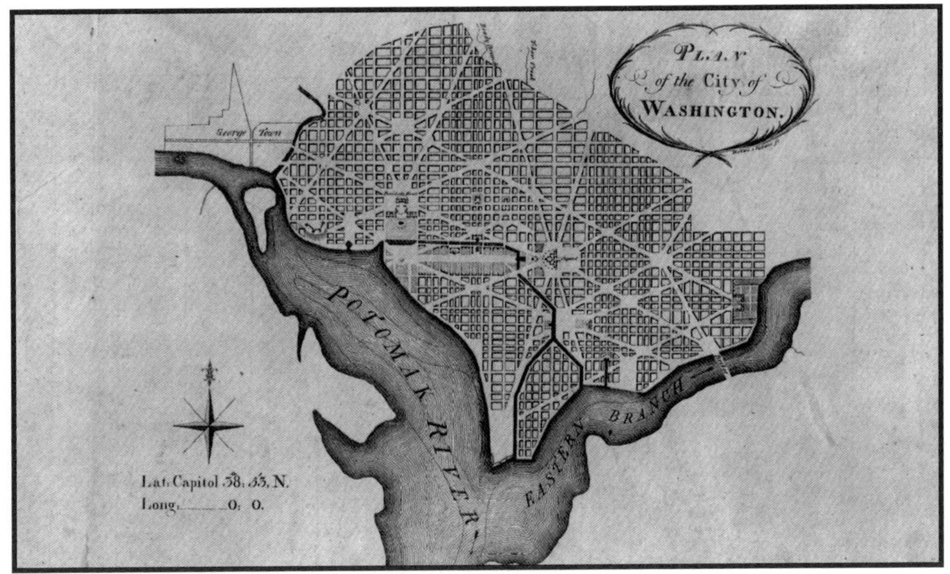

One of the first published drawings of Pierre L'Enfant's plan for the new capital city of the United States. (Library of Congress)

On the slow trip to France, Jones spent time with the ship's captain, Joshua Barney. Barney was a rising captain in the Continental Navy, and the two men became friends. Barney told Jones of his own experiences with poor commanding officers. This included one captain who refused to give Barney the order to fire on an advancing British warship. The captain said he did not have the intention of shedding blood, a curious attitude during wartime. Jones must have been happy that the Continental Navy had other captains in his aggressive mode.

As they approached Europe, Jones had an odd request for his new friend. He asked Barney to steer towards Britain and put him ashore. Jones said he had confidential dispatches for American ambassador John Adams. Barney pointed out that Jones was still a wanted man in Britain, and that if he were captured, he risked being hanged as a pirate. Jones ignored the caution.

Jones spent a few hours in London, passing the dispatches to Adams before heading on to France. One had to wonder if the dispatches were really so urgent as to require such a risk.

Louis XVI graciously received Jones in Paris, but it took Jones nearly a year to get any of the promised money. By then, 1785, the French government was almost as broke as the American government. Financial problems would be one of the main causes of the French Revolution, which would begin in the summer of 1789.

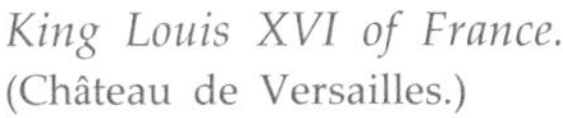

King Louis XVI of France. (Château de Versailles.)

By then, Jones spent much of his free time in Paris tangled in romantic liaisons. There is evidence, although none of it conclusive, that Jones fathered an illegitimate son during this period. He wrote a letter to a woman, Madame Townsend, that mentioned her baby boy and asked her to "cover him all over with kisses from me, they come warm *to you both* from the heart." His usual letters to his girlfriends were flowery, in the style of the time, but much less open and honest.

By the summer of 1787, Jones had returned to New York City, the temporary American capital, still trying unsuccessfully to advance his career. By November, he was heading back to Paris. On the way, he made another secret trip to deliver dispatches to John Adams.

Jones's arrival in Paris was very curious for him. Usually very self-publicizing, this time he slipped into town. He did not even use his proper name in checking into a hotel. He then sent a note to the American ambassador to France, Thomas Jefferson, asking him to a secret meeting. Jones had previously asked Jefferson to help with a girlfriend. If the secret letter dealt with another girlfriend, Jefferson seems to have been able to work the problem out.

Jefferson had his own reasons for seeing Jones. He had a job offer to relay. Jones's reputation had spread all the way to Russia. Catherine the Great, the ruling czarina, wanted to hire him to command a Russian fleet in the Black Sea against the Turkish Empire. Jefferson asked Jones if he wanted a temporary posting to the Russian navy.

Jefferson encouraged Jones to take the position. Russia had been neutral during the American Revolution, and Jefferson probably thought it would be a good diplomatic move that might help to ensure better relations

Catherine the Great, czarina of Russia, requested the services of John Paul Jones to assist in her campaign to defeat the Turks in the Black Sea. (The State Tretyakov Gallery, Moscow)

between the United States and Russia in the future. He told Jones that serving with the Russian Navy would provide training in high command to better prepare for a senior position with the United States Navy, or even command of the Navy—should there ever actually be a navy. By this time, the United States Navy was well on its way to disappearing, and efforts to rebuild it would not start for another decade.

Jones, however, was not initially enthusiastic about going to Russia. He later wrote that he regarded the offer as a "castle in the air." Russia had no naval tradition, and he was warned about the political intrigues of the Russian court. Considering his experience with the far milder politics that had affected the Continental Navy and his own career, Jones was reluctant to repeat the experience.

Jones did not immediately make a decision. He decided to first go to Denmark to recover more prize money he was owed. However, on the day he was supposed to leave Paris for Copenhagen, he had breakfast with the Russian ambassador to France. The ambassador flattered Jones and promised him that within a year he would make the Turkish government in Constantinople tremble. By the time Jones got to Denmark, and he'd begun corresponding personally with Czarina Catherine, he was leaning towards accepting the offer.

Jones did not want to share command. He wrote Catherine, "Being an entire stranger, I have more to fear from a joint authority than any officer in Her Majesty's Service. But I cannot conceive that Her Majesty could deem it expedient to *divide the command* in the Black Sea."

Jones had not commanded a ship in combat for eight years. He was now forty years old and not as vigorous as before. But he was anxious to get back into action, and to again win a reputation as a great naval commander. Besides, he had few other options. He would go to Russia.

In Russia, Jones feuded with the Russian aristocracy worse than he had with the American captains, but he got along very well with the Russian crew members and junior officers. Some of them joined him on one mission, when Jones rowed at night among the Turkish fleet before the second battle of the Liman, when he used chalk to mark ships targeted for attack by the Russian navy.

Jones could exhibit paranoia at times and become convinced that his fellow officers were out to get him. In Russia this was not an illusion. Despite the promises the czarina and the ambassador had made, Jones ended up only commanding part of the fleet fighting the Turks. He also had trouble gaining the cooperation of the other commanders, even when Jones needed it in combat. Nevertheless, the Russian navy won the two battles of the Liman, which were fought in a small bay-like estuary where the Dnieper River flowed into the Black Sea. Jones played a major role in the victory.

Typically, however, Jones lost the political fighting that followed the sea victories. One of his co-commanders was far less useful in the fight than Jones, but he was the protégé of Gregory Potemkin, who was effectively second only to Catherine in power in Russia. When Jones complained about the commander's lack of cooperation and poor performance in battle, he was recalled to the Russian capital of St. Petersburg. There the navy gave him a face-saving command with the Northern Fleet. But in Russia during the long winter months, the Northern Fleet sat dormant. For five months, so did Jones.

In April 1789, Jones was accused of raping a young girl. After some investigation, he was cleared of the charge. It turned out the girl, who was twelve but claimed to be ten, had been paid by someone to say that Jones had attacked her. Jones argued that he had not forced her but that each time she came to see him she had lent herself willingly to "do all that a man would want of her."

Jones avoided the rape conviction because he was able to defend himself by proving that their encounters were consensual. Although he did not stand trial, his career in Russia was finished. He was never given another command, but did receive two years' pay. He left Russia in the summer of 1789.

Jones spent much of the next year wandering around Europe, job hunting. He tried unsuccessfully to get back into Catherine's good graces, with written justifications of his actions in battle and plans for further campaigns. He wrote important people in the United States and even made a trip to London to settle a debt with Edward Bancroft. Apparently, he still did not know that Bancroft had been a British spy. This time a mob recognized Jones and nearly attacked him.

By 1790, he was back in Paris, where he tried to maintain a social life but with little success. He was no longer the romantic and popular figure of ten years before. Furthermore, the French Revolution had started. It was a new era.

Things looked like they might improve for Jones. In the late spring of 1792, Congress finally appointed a commission to negotiate with the governments of North Africa for the release of American sailors that had been seized from merchantmen and held prisoner since. Thomas Jefferson, now secretary of state, had Jones appointed to head the commission. Success here might have put Jones back into the public eye and put his career back on track.

However, on July 18, 1792, a few days before notice of his appointment arrived in Paris, Jones was found dead in his apartment. He had apparently succumbed to pneumonia or a similar lung disease. The French Revolutionary government, which considered him to be a hero for his fight against the British, paid for his funeral.

It took over a century for John Paul Jones to get honors from the American government, as well as recognition of his accomplishments that he fought so hard for in his life. In 1905, President Theodore Roosevelt was building up a strong United States Navy. American military leaders and experts had recognized the importance of sea power. Roosevelt decided that it was time for Jones to be credited with his place in American history. The president had Jones's remains disinterred from a grave in Paris and brought back to America. John Paul Jones's tomb now sits in the U.S. Naval Academy in Annapolis, Maryland.

John Paul Jones was a complicated hero. He was a brave and brilliant naval commander who appeared in the American colonies at the right time to earn his desired place in history. But he was tragically flawed. An unpleasant, self-indulgent self-promoter, it is easy for us today to connect to his frustration at living in a world where ancestry, more than talent, controlled a man's career. But even in today's more meritocratic military, one has to be able to get along with superiors, equals, and subordinates, something he failed at miserably in more than one navy.

Jones was selfish and greedy for fame, and foolishly thought only actions as a naval commander counted. In the process he made too many enemies.

Jones's tomb can be visited at the U.S. Naval Academy in Annapolis, Maryland. (Library of Congress)

The complex and seemingly fearless Captain John Paul Jones remains a legend in American history. (Library of Congress)

What John Paul Jones did do was give America hope during the long, bloody revolution. He was by far the new nation's most successful naval officer. He was willing to "go in harm's way" and also had a strategic vision of how the navy might grow and function. He was an early advocate for a professional navy and that is why history remembers Jones today as the father of the U.S. Navy.

Timeline

1747	Jones is born on July 6.
1760	Becomes apprentice on *Friendship*.
1764	Third mate on the slave ship *King George*.
1766	First mate on the slave ship *Two Friends*.
1768	Mungo Maxwell incident.
1773	Kills "the Ringleader"; flees to America.
1775	Commissioned lieutenant in Continental Navy; second in command of *Alfred*.
1776	Given command of *Providence*; Nova Scotia expedition; captures *Mellish* with cargo of British winter uniforms.
1777	Takes command of *Ranger*; sails for France in November.
1778	Cruises the *Ranger*; raids on Whitehaven and attempt to capture Lord Selkirk unsuccessful; captures *HMS Drake*, becoming first American captain to defeat British ship in one-on-one combat.
1779	Given command of *Bonhomme Richard*; defeats *Serapis* despite *Bonhomme Richard* sinking; given command of *Alliance*.

1781	Back in the United States, Jones is given command of *America*.
1782	The *America* given to the French.
1788	Arrives in St. Petersburg to become admiral in Russian navy.
1789	Framed for sex scandal; leaves Russia in August 1789.
1792	Dies in Paris on July 18.
1905	Body recovered and returned to the United States.

Sources

CHAPTER ONE: Beginnings and Implications

p. 10, "ardent to make . . ." Evan Thomas, *John Paul Jones* (New York: Simon & Schuster, 2003), 14.

p. 13, "that most disheartening . . ." Charles Francis Adams, *Letters of Mrs. Adams* (Boston: Little Brown, 1840), 3.

CHAPTER TWO: Early Maritime Career

p. 26, "neither mortal nor . . ." Samuel Eliot Morison, *John Paul Jones: A Sailor's Biography* (Boston: Little Brown and Company, 1959), 19.

p. 26, "most unmercifully, by the . . ." Ibid.

p. 27, "ungracious conduct to . . ." Thomas, *John Paul Jones,* 26.

p. 28, "he approved himself . . ." Ibid., 27.

p. 31, "a prodigious brute . . ." Ibid., 31.

p. 31, "the grossest abuse . . ." Ibid.

p. 31, "swore with horrid . . ." Ibid.

CHAPTER THREE: War at Sea

p. 35, "Many of the . . ." Nathan Miller, *Sea of Glory* (New York: David McKay Company, Inc., 1974), 4.

p. 43, "The Truth is we . . ." William B. Wilcox and Barbara B. Oberg, eds., *The Papers of Benjamin Franklin* (New Haven, CT: Yale University Press, 1990), 588.

CHAPTER FOUR: The Continental Navy

p. 54, "Any young gentleman . . ." Gordon Wood, *The Radicalism of the American Revolution* (New York: Vintage, 1991), 33.

p. 55, "The learning he . . ." Nathaniel Fanning, *Fanning's Narrative: Being the Memoirs of Nathaniel Fanning An Officer of the Revolutionary Navy, 1778-1783,* ed. John S. Barnes (New York: Naval Historical Society, 1912), 106.

p. 55, "I should have . . ." Jones to Robert Morris, Dec. 11, 1777, in *Naval Documents of the American Revolution,* vol. 10, ed. William Bell Clark (Washington, DC: Naval Historical Center, 1964-1996).

p. 58, "the maddest idea . . ." Thomas, *John Paul Jones,* 43.

p. 58, "represented the most . . ." Nathan Miller, *Broadsides: The Age of Fighting Sail, 1775-1815* (New York: John Wiley and Sons, 2000), 20.

p. 59, "building at the . . ." Thomas, *John Paul Jones,* 43.

p. 63, "It was I who . . ." Gerard W. Gawalt, ed., *John Paul Jones's Memoirs of the American Revolution Presented to King Louis XVI of France* (Washington, DC: Library of Congress, 1979), 6.

p. 64, "I formed an exercise . . ." Thomas, *John Paul Jones,* 52.

p. 64, "It is certainly . . ." Morison, *John Paul Jones: A Sailor's Biography,* 52.

p. 68, "The loss of the . . ." Thomas, *John Paul Jones,* 71.

CHAPTER FIVE: To France

p. 70-71, "King's officer . . ." Thomas, *John Paul Jones,* 76.

p. 71, "That such despicable . . ." Ibid., 77.

p. 72, "is a fine fellow . . ." Jones, *Naval Documents of the American Revolution,* 1092.

p. 72, "always entertaining . . ." Thomas, *John Paul Jones,* 78.

p. 72, "It has always . . ." Ibid.
p. 74, "fine frigate," Ibid., 87.
p. 78, "Our captain took . . ." Jones, *Naval Documents of the American Revolution,* 1092.
p. 78, "Had he suspected . . ." Ibid.
p. 80, "Were this base . . ." Thomas, *John Paul Jones,* 96.
p. 81-82, "It is with great . . ." Ibid., 99.
p. 84, "When an enemy . . ." Ibid., 112.

CHAPTER SIX: The Cruise of the *Ranger*
p. 88, "a slow and half . . ." Thomas, *John Paul Jones,* 114.
p. 91, "people were unwilling . . ." Ezra Green, *Diary of Ezra Green, M.D.,* eds. George Henry Preble and Walter C. Green (New York: Arno Press, 1971), 21.
p. 95, "The inhabitants began . . ." Thomas, *John Paul Jones,* 123.
p. 96, "Upon the whole . . ." Anna De Koven, *The Life and Letters of John Paul Jones,* vol. 1 (New York: Scribner's, 1930), 309.
p. 96, "It was immediately . . ." Ibid.
p. 97, "The tide and what . . ." Green, *Diary of Ezra Green, M.D.,* 20.

CHAPTER SEVEN: The *Bonhomme Richard*
p. 103, "have no connection . . ." Morison, *John Paul Jones: A Sailor's Biography,* 182.
p. 105, "jealous of everything . . ." John Adams, *Diary and Autobiography of John Adams,* vol. 2, eds. L. H. Butterfield and Richard Alan Ryerson. (Cambridge, MA: Belknap, 1963), 168.
p. 107, "was determined to . . ." Thomas, *John Paul Jones,* 170.
p. 107, "That's a damn . . ." Ibid., 170.
p. 109, "It is the opinion . . ." Morison, *John Paul Jones: A Sailor's Biography,* 145.

p. 109, "They are certainly . . ." Ibid.

CHAPTER EIGHT: "I Have Not Yet Begun to Fight"

p. 114, "As soon as Jones . . ." Fanning, *Fanning's Narrative,* 33.

p. 117, "The captains of the . . ." Ibid., 37.

p. 118, "Tell me instantly . . ." Thomas, *John Paul Jones,* 183.

p. 119, "She made a dreadful . . ." Fanning, *Fanning's Narrative,* 40.

p. 119-120, "I must confess that . . ." Thomas, *John Paul Jones,* 186.

p. 124, "Quarters . . ." Ibid., 191-192.

CHAPTER NINE: The Letdown

p. 128-129, "Paul Jones resembles . . ." Thomas, *John Paul Jones,* 199.

p. 130, "During the engagement . . ." Ibid., 200.

p. 131, "great friends . . . " Ibid., 205-206.

p. 134, "If you had stayed . . ." Benjamin Franklin, *Papers of Benjamin Franklin,* vol. 78, eds. William B. Wilcox and Barbara B. Oberg (New Haven, CT: Yale University Press, 1986), 78.

p. 138, "cover him all over . . ." Thomas, *John Paul Jones,* 264.

p. 140, "castle in the air," Ibid., 267.

p. 141, "Being an entire . . ." Ibid., 268.

p. 142, "do all that . . ." Ibid., 298.

Bibliography

Adams, Charles Francis. *Letters of Mrs. Adams.* Boston: Little Brown, 1840.

Adams, John. *Diary and Autobiography of John Adams.* Edited by L. H. Butterfield and Richard Alan Ryerson. Vol. 2. Cambridge, MA: Belknap, 1963.

Allen, Gardner W. *A Naval History of the American Revolution.* Boston: Houghton, 1913.

Anderson, Fred. *Crucible of War.* New York: Vintage Books, 2000.

Bowen-Hassell, E. Gordon, Dennis M. Conrad, and Mark L. Hayes. *Sea Raiders of the American Revolution: The Continental Navy in European Waters,* Washington, DC:Department of the Navy, Naval Historical Center, 2003.

Clark, William Bell, et al, editors. *Naval Documents of the American Revolution.* 10 vols. 1966-2004.

De Koven, Anna. *The Life and Letters of John Paul Jones.* Vol. 1. New York: Scribner's, 1930.

Fanning, Nathaniel. *Fanning's Narrative: Being the Memoirs of Nathaniel Fanning An Officer of the Revolutionary Navy, 1778-1783.* Edited by John S. Barnes. New York: Naval Historical Society, 1912.

Fehrenbacher, Don E. *The Slaveholding Republic.* Completed and edited by Ward M. McAfee. New York: Oxford University Press, 2001.

Fowler, William M. Jr. *Rebels Under Sail.* New York: Charles Scribner's Sons, 1976.

Franklin, Benjamin. *Papers of Benjamin Franklin.* Edited by William B. Wilcox and Barbara B. Oberg. New Haven, CT: Yale University Press, 1986, 1992-1997.

Gawalt, Gerard W., ed. *John Paul Jones's Memoirs of the American Revolution Presented to King Louis XVI of France.* Washington, DC: Library of Congress, 1979

Green, Ezra. *Diary of Ezra Green, M.D.* Edited by George Henry Preble and Walter C. Green. New York: Arno Press, 1971.

Leckie, Robert. *George Washington's War.* New York: HarperCollins, 1992.

Miller, Nathan. *Broadsides.* New York: John Wiley & Sons, Inc., 2000.

———. *Sea of Glory.* New York: David McKay Company, Inc., 1974.

Morison, Samuel Eliot. *John Paul Jones: A Sailor's Biography.* Boston: Little Brown and Company, An Atlantic Monthly Book, 1959.

Thomas, Evan. "Evan Thomas on John Paul Jones." Interviewed by J. Dennis Robinson. SeacoastNH.com. www.seacoastnh.com/maritime_history/John_Paul_Jones/Evan_Thomas_on_John_Paul_Jones/ (Accessed November 2005).

———. *John Paul Jones.* New York: Simon & Schuster, 2003.

Tuchman, Barbara W. *The First Salute.* New York: Alfred A. Knopf, 1988.

Walsh, John Evangelist. *Night on Fire: The First Complete Account of John Paul Jones's Greatest Battle.* New York: McGraw-Hill, 1978.

Wood, Gordon. *The Radicalism of the American Revolution.* New York: Vintage, 1991.

http://www.usna.edu/LibExhibits/JohnPaulJones/Jpj_main.html

John Paul Jones's crypt is on the grounds of the U.S. Naval Academy, where a marine honor guard watches over it during visiting hours. The USNA's library maintains a virtual exhibit devoted to Jones, including links to other resources and scans of two letters—one from George Washington to Jones, the other from Jones himself.

http://www.jpj.demon.co.uk/

The cottage in which Jones was born, in Scotland, is maintained as a museum. Exhibits include a scale model of the *Bonhomme Richard.*

http://www.pbs.org/benfranklin/

A PBS site devoted to the life and times of Benjamin Franklin.

www.history.navy.mil

This site provides official historical information concerning the U.S. Navy, including wars, conflicts, individual ship histories, and photos.

http://www.pbs.org/ktca/liberty/
PBS produced an award-winning documentary series, *Liberty!,* about the American Revolution.

http://www.lhd6.navy.mil/
These pages from the navy's Web site are devoted to the ship *Bonhomme Richard.* Though John Paul Jones's vessel sank in 1779, the navy has a new *Bonhomme Richard,* an amphibious assault ship commissioned in 1998.

Index